ROME WALKS

ON FOOT GUIDES

ROME WALKS

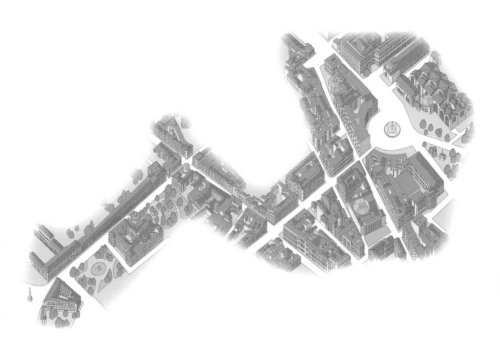

John Fort & Rachel Piercey

DUNCAN PETERSEN

gpp®
travel

Conceived, designed and produced by
Duncan Petersen Publishing Limited
C7, Old Imperial Laundry
Warriner Gardens, London SW11 4XW
United Kingdom

Published in the USA by
Globe Pequot Press
Guilford, Connecticut

UK ISBN-13: 978-1-903301-58-6
US ISBN: 978-0-7627-6110-4

A CIP catalogue record for this book is available from the British Library.
Library of Congress Cataloging-in-Publication Data is available.

Conceived, designed and produced by
Duncan Petersen Publishing Ltd

Editorial Director Andrew Duncan

Editors Jo Beckett-King, Tara O'Sullivan

Maps Global Mapping Ltd, Mapping Company Ltd, Oxford Designers and Illustrators

Photographs John Fort, Rachel Piercey

Printed by Edelvives Talleres Graficos, Spain

Visit Duncan Petersen's travel website at
www.charmingsmallhotels.co.uk

CONTENTS

Exploring Rome on foot

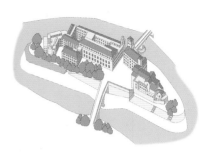

Rome is unique among the 'art' cities of Italy due to its size and fascinating history, which spans more than 2,700 years. It is much larger and older than Venice or Florence: they both date from the Middle Ages, while Rome dates back to its founding in 753 BC. This is the date given by Roman historians and served as the starting point for Roman dating (AUC, *Ab Urbe Condita*, From the Founding of the City), and modern archaeology confirms that the origins of the city go back to about then. As the centre of the largest empire in the world for some of those centuries and of Christianity from its infancy, the city was either rich, or extremely rich for much of that time. It attracted many of the greatest and most inventive artists and architects, with the result that there is a range of monuments and buildings, sculptures and paintings, fountains and squares of a quantity, quality, beauty and variety not to be found anywhere else in the world. There are fine temples from 100 BC and striking modern buildings from the 21st century (although not many, admittedly), and in between an enormous variety of extraordinary creations, with something from every single century. However, all this poses difficulties to the visitor, because distances across the historic centre are considerable, and unless the stay is quite long, it is necessary to make the difficult decision of what to see and what not.

HOW THE MAPPING WAS MADE

A small team of specialist cartographers created the maps digitally in Adobe Illustrator. The footprint of the buildings is drawn first, then the width of the streets is artificially increased in order to give extra space for the buildings to be drawn in three dimensions. Next, the buildings are added, using aerial photography as reference. Finally the details of the buildings and the colour is added - the first very time consuming, the second less so because digital drawing programmes allow it to be automated.

The walks in this book are designed to help with just that.

It is very much a city for walking, but you should careful to eke out your stamina and physical resources as you move around. In addition to the distances to be covered, it is important to remember the famous seven hills on which Rome is built – actually eight if we include the Janiculum (**The Other Romans,** page 120), not counted among the original seven because it is on the west side of

the Tiber. Although the hills are not high, they are at many points quite steep, and you will find yourself at times confronted with long uphill stretches and often by rather daunting flights of steps or ramps. Also, very little of the centre of the city has been made permanently pedestrian, which means that while admiring some exquisite architectural detail you must always keep a watchful eye on the somewhat relentless traffic. However, such is the concentration throughout the city of beautiful squares, fountains, monuments, churches and works of art, there is always plenty to inspire. The metro system is limited, but can be of use getting to and from starting points. The bus system is comprehensive and worth getting to grips with.

The twelve walks have been carefully chosen to give as wide a selection as possible in terms of chronology and variety of form, and include many of the best-known sights and monuments as well as a wealth of less famous, but no less interesting, ones. The titles are thematic (e.g. 'Baroque Splendour'), but one of the fascinations of the city is the constant juxtaposition of monuments from centuries far apart, or of buildings created out of Roman remains – or indeed just piled on top of them – which means that the walk may well go off on tangents from the basic theme. The itineraries are designed to be covered in about two hours, but this is on the assumption that you do not allow yourself to deviate or be distracted. This may well be too much to expect, and the likelihood is that you will find yourself enticed away from following the route strictly by some vista or intriguing courtyard, or a particularly well-placed bar – the coffee in Rome is universally excellent. In which case, the walk may well last much longer.

Of paramount importance as you move around the city is to look upwards, constantly. This is not just to admire the rooftop terraces from which vegetation spills evocatively – no flat space is wasted in the city – but to admire the fine architectural features of so many of the buildings: the giant wooden doors; the intricately carved stone window frames and cornices; the beautiful colours of the façades; the little shrines perching on the corners of so many blocks. Also look ahead at the endless changing vistas, many accidental but many intentional. There is a strong theatrical element to the city, particularly in those parts dating from the 17th and 18th centuries, when architects deliberately exploited the differences of level in the city to create panoramas and surprises round corners.

It will be noticed that there is one major omission in the book, the Vatican Museums, Sistine Chapel and St Peter's. This was not an easy decision to make, as clearly the Vatican is one of the key attractions of Rome, but it was felt such a concentration of things to see in a small area could hardly be treated as a walk in the style of the other ones, and if done properly would have resulted in something very unwieldy and out of proportion for a book of this size.

If you manage to do all twelve walks, you will have a good grounding in what the city has to offer, and will have been introduced to all its main delights (except the Vatican) and many others too. The hope is that this book will help you acquire a taste for the city and that you will be back for more, but as the distinguished Italian journalist, Silvio Negro (1897 – 1959) said, 'Rome, a lifetime is not enough'.

Trajan's Market.

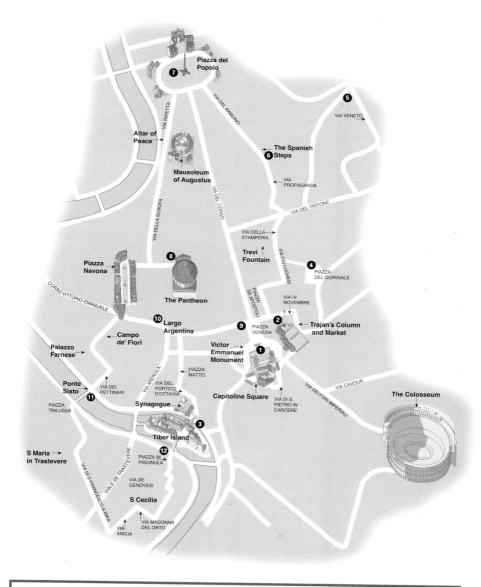

Piazza del
Popolo

VIA DEL BABUINO

VIA RIPETTA

VIA VENETO

Altar of
Peace

The Spanish
Steps

Mausoleum
of Augustus

VIA
PROPAGANDA

VIA DELLA SCROFA

VIA DEL CORSO

VIA DEL TRITONE

VIA DELLA
STAMPERIA

Trevi
Fountain

VIA DEI LUCCHESI

PIAZZA
DEL QUIRINALE

Piazza
Navona

The Pantheon

CORSO VITTORIO EMANUELE

PIAZZA SS APOSTOLI

VIA IV
NOVEMBRE

Largo
Argentina

Campo
de' Fiori

PIAZZA
VENEZIA

Trajan's Column
and Market

Victor
Emmanuel
Monument

Palazzo
Farnese

VIA AREÑULA

PIAZZA
MATTEI

VIA DEI FORI IMPERIALI

VIA CAVOUR

The Colosseum

Ponte
Sisto

VIA DEI
PETTINARI

VIA DEL
PORTICO
D'OTTAVIA

Capitoline Square

VIA DI S.
PIETRO IN
CARCERE

PIAZZA
TRILUSSA

Synagogue

Tiber Island

S Maria
in Trastevere

VIA DI S FRANCESCO A RIPA

VIALE DE TRASTEVERE

PIAZZA IN
PISCINULA

VIA DE
GENOVESI

S Cecilia

VIA
ANICIA

VIA MADONNA
DEL ORTO

HOW TO USE THIS BOOK

The area covered by the walks stretches from Piazza del Popolo in the north to Trastevere in the south, and from Ponte Sisto in the west to Via Veneto and the Colosseum in the east.

Using the maps

The route of each walk is clearly marked on the map, with the occasional arrow to keep you heading in the right direction. This guide tells you where the walk starts and finishes, as well as giving the name of the nearest metro station. If the nearest metro station is a significant distance away, the guide gives an indication of how far away it is, to help you plan your day.

Numerals on the maps correspond to the numerals in the text, marking the start of each section of the walk. Street names are shown in bold print, as are places of interest such as buildings, museums, galleries, statues, sculptures, restaurants, cafés, or shops.

LINKING THE WALKS

Because of the high concentration of things to see in the centre of the city, several of the walks run close to each other or even cross over at points. If you have the energy to complete one walk and then move on to another, or interweave parts of two walks, there are various combinations that could be considered. For instance, **The Heart, Soul and Guts of Ancient Rome** ends very close to the beginning of **Two Islands**, and the two would give a broad and contrasting selection of what the city offers. Or **Two Islands** leads very naturally into **The Other Romans**. The same could be said of **La Dolce Vita** and **Baroque Splendour**, although these two are quite demanding physically and involve going up and down some of the steepest parts of town more than once. The four walks, **Lost in the Folds of History**, **In the Footsteps of Caravaggio**, **Life at the Top** and **As Roman as it Comes** are completely intertwined, but involving no hills could perhaps be coupled in any sort of combination. For the very fit and for those with limited time it would in fact be perfectly feasible to do three of these walks in unbroken succession, but perhaps not advisable on account of the risk of cultural indigestion. **Counts and Pilgrims** leads off from near where **The Other Romans** ends and the two go very well together and there are no hills. In fact, with an early start, there is another challenge for the for the fit and hurried, the threesome of **Two Islands**, **The Other Romans** and finally **Counts and Pilgrims**.

WHEN TO USE THIS BOOK

From the point of view of the weather, it
makes no difference to these walks whether
they are done in summer or winter – they
are equally suited to both. But from the
point of view of the crowds, the city is
exceedingly busy from Easter until well into
the autumn, with the months of May, June,
July, the second half of September and the
whole of October being especially crowded.
There is a particular crush at the Colosseum,
Spanish Steps, Trevi Fountain, Pantheon and
Piazza Navona, and those hating throngs
should bear this in mind when following
**Living Archaeology, La Dolce Vita,
Romantics and Retail, Lost in the Folds of
History** and **Counts and Pilgrims** during
the summer. In most of the rest of the city
crowds are rarely a problem even at the
height of the season, but **The Other
Romans** is the walk which offers the best
escape from multitudes.

WEEKEND WALKS

On Saturdays during much of the year many
of Rome's most beautiful churches are in use
for weddings, and are therefore
decorated with especially fine
and extravagant arrangements
of flowers. The following
walks include churches that
are particularly popular:

• **The Heart, Soul and Guts
of Ancient Rome:** S. Maria in
Aracoeli is very much in
demand. The main doors are
opened and the bride climbs
the 124 steps to the top.

• **Living Archaeology:** Santi
Giovanni e Paolo is also very
popular, as it is set in a quiet
square, and has the advantage
of easy parking.

• **Baroque Splendour:**
Bernini's exquisite S. Andrea al
Quirinale is perfectly suited to
more intimate ceremonies.

THE WEATHER

The average rain fall in Rome is higher
than that of London, but this is because
when it rains, it rains – it very rarely
drizzles. However, overall there is more
sunshine and temperatures are much more
clement. Winters are on the whole chilly
rather than cold, but can drop below 0°
with a cutting wind (the hated
tramontana) and icicles on fountains, but
usually not for very long. February and
November are regarded as particularly
wet months by Romans, but in fact you
can get soaked in a good storm at any
time of year. The hottest period is usually
the second half of July, almost always
with at least one peak of 40°, but the
whole of July and at least the first two
weeks of August are hotter than most
people like. April – June and September –
October are much more mellow, but on
fine days even in the middle of winter it
is often possible to sit outside for lunch
on the sunny side of a square. For the
discerning visitor the meteorological risks
of coming in winter are far outweighed
by the many fewer tourists in the city.

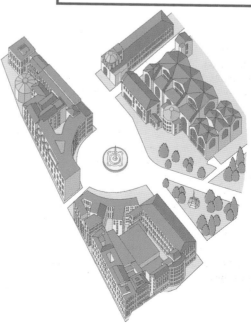

• **Lost in the Folds of History:** S. Agnese is perfect for not at all intimate ceremonies.

• **The Other Romans:** S. Cecilia is set in peace and quiet, is large and light and has the great advantage of its garden and courtyard where children can play as the knot is tied.

Provided the visitor is discreet, churches can almost always be visited during weddings.

On Sundays there are services, sometimes several, in all these churches, and then access may not be possible to certain parts of the church. This particularly matters in S. Maria del Popolo (**In the Footsteps of Caravaggio**) as you cannot see the paintings during the service.

WEEKDAY WALKS

In answer to tourism, nearly everything in the city works seven days a week. However, on Mondays most Italian state museums are closed, which includes the Capitoline Museums in **The Heart, Soul and Guts**, Palazzo Barberini in **La Dolce Vita**, the Altar of Peace in **In the Footsteps of Caravaggio**, Palazzo Altemps in **Lost in the Folds of History**, the Museo Barracco in **As Roman as it Comes** and the Galleria Corsini in **The Other Romans**. However, this does not affect the Colosseum and Forum area, which are open every day of the year except Christmas day, so you should not have trouble with **Living Archaeology**.

WALKS FOR KIDS

Rome is quite hard for children, but most of them relish anything that smacks of death. The walks below offer a sample.

• **Living Archaeology**: this takes you past the Colosseum, in which the entertainment was principally the shedding of blood – humans against humans, humans against animals or animals against animals. The associations of the place are enough to rouse the curiosity of almost all children, although adults often find the monument rather sinister, soaked as it is human suffering. This walk also takes in the Palatine Hill, where there are endless slopes to run up and down, tunnels to explore, and ruins and lumps of masonry on which to climb.

• **La Dolce Vita**: the church of S. Maria della Concezione, with its ingenious arrangements of bones, product of some monk's macabre sense of humour, is always a success with children. At the end of the walk is the spectacular Trevi Fountain, which delights all ages, and is surrounded by ice-cream parlours, convenient for dispensing rewards for good behaviour.

GETTING TO ROME

Rome has two airports, Fiumicino and Ciampino, which are both well served by national and budget airlines. Most budget and charter flights arrive at Ciampino airport. It is also possible to travel to Rome from the UK by train. Take the Eurostar from London to Paris and connect with the overnight sleeper service, which takes 15 hours and 20 minutes.

GETTING AROUND

By far the best way to get around Rome is on foot. The city centre (*Centro Storico*), where most of the major sites are to be found, is fairly compact – it is about 2.5 km from the Colosseum to Piazza di Spagna. However, crowded streets, cobbles, weariness and the heat of the summer means that alternative forms of transport are often welcome. Rome's extensive public transport system of buses, metro, tram and trains is run by the ATAC.

Tickets

Depending on your needs and itinerary, you can buy: a single ticket (Biglietto integrato a tempo, or B.I.T.) for €1, which is valid for 75 minutes on buses or trams, with unlimited transfers, or for one metro ride; a one-day ticket (Biglietto giornaliero or B.I.G.) for €4, valid on all forms of public transport; or a three-day ticket (Biglietto per 3 giorni, or B.T.I.) for €11, which is again valid on all public transport. Purchase your tickets before you begin your journey at metro stations (*tabbachi* – look for a 'T' sign), newspaper stands, vending machines or larger bus stops. Bear in mind that vending machines usually give a maximum of €4 change, so make sure you carry smaller notes or coins with you if you wish to purchase tickets. Be sure to validate your ticket at the entrance to the metro or in the yellow boxes on the bus or tram.

Metro

Rome's underground system was built by Mussolini. It has two main lines: A (orange), and B (blue). They run across the city in two diagonal lines, bisecting at Termini station. Trains run every seven to ten minutes, beginning at 5.30am and stopping at 11.30pm (or 12.30am on Saturdays). As we went to press, line B was closing at the earlier time of 9.00pm every evening except Saturday, due to construction work on the new line C. This is expected to last until at least 2012. Replacement buses are in operation after 9.00pm.

Taxis

Always use registered taxis, which are white or yellow with a Comune di Roma shield on the door. It is usually best to use a taxi rank – if you phone for a taxi, the meter runs from the moment the driver sets off to pick you up. If you're carrying luggage, expect to pay a surcharge of €1 for each item. Fares for the airports are fixed, and at the time of going to press should be €30 for Ciampino and €40 for Fiumincino from the city centre. For all other journeys, take the fare from the meter, rounding it up to the nearest euro. To call a taxi in Rome, try Radio Taxi Samarcanda on 06 66 61, Pronto Taxi on 06 66 45, and La Capitale Radio-Taxi on 06 49 94.

Emergency Police: 113
Carabinieri: 112
Fire: 115
Road Assistance: 116
Medical Emergencies: 118
International Inquiries: 176
Phone Directory Assistance: 12
In a medical emergency tourists can seek multilingual assistance at the *Guardia Turistica*, Nuova Regina Hospital, Via Morosini 30, in Trastevere (Monday to Friday, 8am-8pm).
For less urgent medical help out of hours, or on public holidays, visit one of the many *Pronto Soccorso* (First Aid Centres) in Rome (open 24 hours, 365 days a year). Consult the extensive list at www.romaturismo.it.
Ospedale Pediatrico Bambino Gesù Gianicolo, Piazza S. Onofrio 4, dispenses first aid to children: 06 685 9257.

Buses and trams

Your visit will run more smoothly if you take the time to familiarise yourself with a map of the city and the main bus routes before your arrival in Rome. You can download a map of the city's bus routes at www.atac.roma.it. Alternatively, pick up a map from the ATAC booth outside Termini station. Buses run from 5.50am until midnight, with night buses (stops marked with an owl) taking over for the intervening hours from 12.30 am to 5.30am. The main terminals are Piazza dei Cinquecento (Termini) and Piazza Venezia. Night buses depart every 30 minutes to all parts of the city. On the stop information sign at a bus stop, the name of the stop is enclosed in a red box. The stops listed below it show the bus's onward route. If the destination you want is listed above the red box you will need to go to the stop on the opposite side of the road and catch the bus there.

Although an extensive bus and night bus network covers the city, heavy traffic means that at times buses make slow progress. If you are planning to stay outside the city centre consider looking for accommodation on the route of the metro so you can reach the centre quickly and easily. On Sundays and public holidays, and during August, the number of buses in circulation halves.

Bicycles

Rome is notorious for its traffic congestion. The city's Bike Sharing scheme is a handy way to beat the queues if you are not put off by steep hills and cobbles. Cycling is most enjoyable on Sundays when much of the city centre is closed to traffic. It's also worth renting a bike for a leisurely spin around Rome's parks and gardens. To use the scheme, you'll need to register, purchase a rechargeable smart card (€5.00) and obtain maps of bike sharing locations. The service operates from 7am to 11pm. The first half hour is free, and the cost is €0.50 thereafter. For more information, see www.bikesharing.roma.it.

TOURIST INFORMATION

Rome is well served by public and private tourist information offices and websites.
• **Rome Tourist Board: APT** (Azienda Provinciale per Il turismo di Roma) 06 48 89 91, Via Parigi 5. The APT also has branches at main travel terminals.
• **P.I.T/Tourist Information points** (Punti Informativi Turistici) Open daily, these green kiosks found at points across the city and in the main transport terminals are some of the best places to get information. Multilingual staff can give advice as well as reserving and selling tickets for major attractions. You can also buy tickets for Tiber Boat Tours (see **Boat trips** below), 110 Hop on/Hop off bus and the Archeobus (see **Bus tours** below), and tourist passes. If you have booked a Roma Pass online, this is where you will come to pick it up.

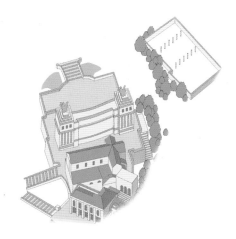

• **Enjoy Rome** (www.enjoyrome.com) Via Marghera 8a, Tel: 06 445 1843, is an independent tourist office staffed entirely by English speakers. It has a helpful website and can book a wide variety of city tours and accommodation.

Travelling with children

For information on events and attractions for children, visit www.romaturismo.it, which also has interactive children's pages filled with tips and suggestions for days out, plus advice for parents.

Disabled travellers

Rome's cobbled streets, crowded pavements and swirling traffic present many challenges to the disabled visitor. Many of the stops on metro line B have lifts, but very few on line A do. It is best to check before you travel. The 590 bus follows the same route as line A and, like most of Rome's buses and trams, is equipped to carry wheelchairs.

Most of Rome's museums are at least partially accessible, although the city's ancient sites are hard to negotiate without assistance. Admission to the Colosseum is free for disabled visitors and carers – bypass the queue and go to the second window to obtain a ticket.

• Comune di Roma's useful bi-lingual website, www.handyturismo.it, offers detailed information on disabled access to major tourist sites and museums, as well as listing restaurants, bars and lavatories that are wheelchair accessible. Handyturismo can also be contacted on 06 3507 3153, from 9am to 5pm, Monday to Friday.

• Rome Accessibile is a useful guide published by CO.IN Sociale. It covers disabled access to Rome's transport, services and attractions. See www.coinsociale.it or telephone 06 2326 7504.

Bus tours

A bus tour can give you a good overview of the city.The 110 Hop on/Hop off open top bus starts and ends at Piazza dei Cinquecento (Termini station), passing about 40 of the most famous sights of Rome with stops at: Quirinale, the Colosseum, Bocca della verita, Piazza Venezia, Piazza

Navona, St Peter's Square, Piazza Cavour, Ara Pacis, the Trevi Fountain, and Via Veneto. It takes about two hours to cover the entire route. An all–day ticket allows you to get on and off as often as you like. The Archeobus, which departs every 20 minutes from Cinquecento Square, stops at the key Roman archaeological sights along the Appian way (Circo Massimo, Mura Aureliane, San Callisto and San Sebastiano catacombs, Tempio di Romolo, Circo di Massenzio, Mausoleo di Cecilia Metella, Villa dei Quintili, Mausoleo di Casal Rotondo, Valle della Caffarella, Baths of Caracalla, etc). Both services offer an on board commentary in several languages, and it is possible to buy a joint ticket for both buses.

A cheaper way to get an overview of Rome is on the number 19 tram, (Piazza Risorgimento — Piazza Porta Maggiore) or the number 3 from Valle Giulia (near the Zoo) to the Stazione Trastevere.

Boat trips

Tourist boats on the Tiber sail between Ponte Duca d'Aosta and Isola Tiberina stopping at points in between. Hour–long guided cruises begin from Castel Sant'Angelo, and all–day cruises taking in Ostia Antica leave from Ponte Marconi on Friday, Saturday and Sunday. See www.battellidiroma.it.

Museum entry

Rome is invariably crowded, so forward planning will make for a much more enjoyable trip. Purchasing a tourist pass, such as the Roma Pass, is a good idea. The Roma Pass is valid for three days, and entitles the holder to: unlimited journeys on public transport; free admissions to two museums or sites (from a list of 38); reduced admission prices on subsequent museum visits; discounted tickets for cultural events; and access to health care assistance. As we went to press, the Roma Pass cost €25. There are several other tourist passes, including the Archeologia Card, the Museo Nazionale Romano Card, and the Appia Antica Card, all offering different benefits.

TIPPING

Service is usually included in the price (look for *servizio* on the bill), but it is customary to leave something on the table after you have paid your bill if you are particularly pleased with the service. If your restaurant bill does not include service, add 10-15%. In cafés and bars, tips are not expected although it is usual to leave a few coins. It is always less expensive to stand at a bar to consume your drink or snack than sit at a table. Pay first and give the receipt to the barman with your order.

Opening hours

All state-run museums are closed on Mondays (with the exception of the Colosseum and the Baths of Caracalla), so plan your itinerary accordingly. Almost all museums are closed on 25 December, 1 January and 1 May. Major museums are usually open from 9.30am to 7pm, with last admission one hour before closing. The large archaeological sites open at 9am and close one hour before sunset. Remember that the Vatican City is independent of Rome and keeps its own schedules.

Lost property

The Comune di Roma office for lost property (*oggetti smarriti*) is at Circonvallazione Ostiense 191, phone 06 67 69 32 14. It is open Monday to Friday from 8am to 6.30pm. In the event of lost or stolen ID, you must file a report at the Police or *Carabinieri* Station closest to where it went missing. If you lose your passport, contact your consulate or embassy in Italy. There are left luggage facilities at Termini station beneath platform 24.

Shopping and banking hours

Shops in the centre of Rome are generally open from around 9am to around 8pm from Monday to Saturday. Some larger shops open on Sundays. Smaller, family-run businesses usually open from 9am to 1pm and then 3.30pm to 7.30pm. Many shops are closed on Monday mornings, and food shops often close on Thursday afternoons. Most shops will be shut on public holidays, and many shops and restaurants close for two weeks during August.

Banks are open Monday to Friday from 8.30am to 1.30pm and from 3.00pm to 4.30pm. Some banks also open on Saturday mornings. All are shut on Sundays and public holidays. ATMs (*bancomat*) are found all over the city.

You can change your money in banks, at post offices (which usually offer the best rates), or at a *cambio* (exchange office). Post offices are usually open from 8am to 1.45pm Monday to Saturday, but some are open later.

Public holidays

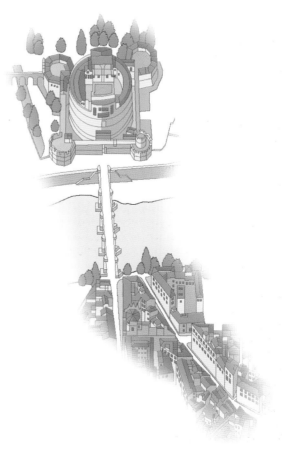

- 1 January (New Year's Day)
- 6 January (Epiphany)
- Easter Sunday
- Easter Monday
- 25 April (Liberation Day)
- 1 May (Labour Day)
- 2 June (Anniversary
of the Republic)
- 29 June (Saints Peter and
Paul – Rome only)
- 15 August (Assumption
of the Virgin)
- 1 November (All
Saints' Day)
- 8 December (Day of the
Immaculate Conception)
- 25 December
(Christmas Day)
- 26 December (Boxing Day
– known in Italy as
Santo Stefano)

Introducing Rome on Foot

This long itinerary is designed to give an overall picture of Rome and will be of use both to those who only have one day in the city and to those who want to get an idea of the place before embarking on a more detailed acquaintance. This introductory walk includes all the famous monuments and sights and also some of the lesser-known ones that feature in the detailed itineraries. It will take the best part of a day to complete and is quite demanding physically, as the distance covered is considerable and the route will lead up and down several of Rome's seven hills.

Looking at the city on foot is certainly the best way to appreciate it, but if a whole day on foot is too daunting or if you have children in tow, it might be wise to take one of the open-top bus tours, particularly bus no. 110, which cover the major points of the whole city.

Start by walking round the **Colosseum**, the most recognizable of ancient Roman monuments, and then walk down the left side of the **Via dei Fori Imperiali** towards the **Piazza Venezia**. After some 200 m, you will see on the high brick wall at the side of the road handsome maps, put up by Mussolini and showing the Roman empire at various stages of its development. At its greatest extent it was astounding, stretching from the borders of Scotland right over to the Persian Gulf. On to the end of this road, and take a diversion over to the right to look at **Trajan's Column** and **Market (Living Archaeology**, page 34). From here you also have a good view of the **Victor Emmanuel Monument (The Heart, Soul and Guts of Ancient Rome**, page 24). Retrace your steps slightly, back over the Via dei Fori Imperiali, and make your way up **Via di S. Pietro in Carcere** to the top, crossing the end of Michelangelo's magnificent **Capitoline Square**. Turn left round the side of the building with the handsome double staircase (**Palazzo Senatorio**), you will come to a vantage point from which you will have a splendid panorama of the **Forum** and **Palatine Hill**.

Head back across the Capitoline Square, towards the two enormous marble figures holding horses (Castor and Pollux). Go down the ramp and bear right, aiming for the far right hand corner of the Piazza Venezia. Here starts the **Via Quattro Novembre**, and almost immediately on the far side of this opens the long and narrow **Piazza Santi Apostoli** (**Life at the Top**, page 96) with the **Palazzo Balestra** at the bottom, where Bonnie Prince Charlie was born. Take the **Via del Vaccaro** to the right, cross the **Piazza della Pilotta** and take the **Via dei Lucchesi** on the far corner, and then the **Via di S. Vincezo**, keeping straight as far as the **Trevi Fountain (La Dolce Vita**, page 64). Relax for a minute here, because, although probably very crowded, it is extraordinarily beautiful. Then take the **Via della Stamperia** on the right side of the fountain. Cross the busy **Via del Tritone**, down the

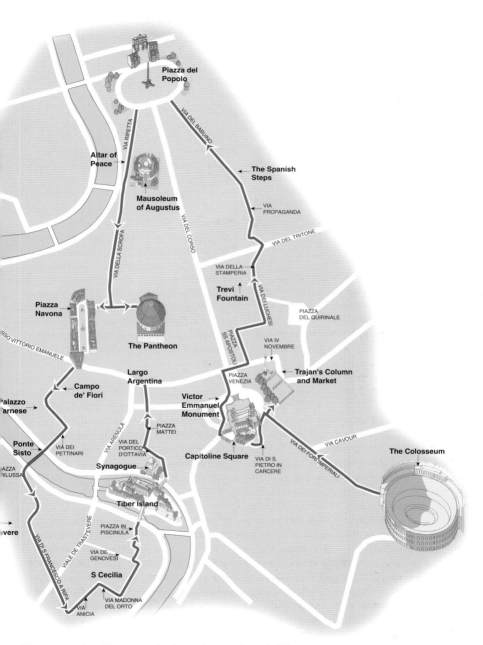

Please note that this map only shows key roads and sights.

Via del Nazareno, through the **Largo Nazareno**, up the **Via di S. Andrea delle Fratte**, across the **Via della Mercede** and down the **Via di Propaganda Fide**, through the **Piazza Mignanelli,** and into the **Piazza di Spagna** and the **Spanish Steps (Romantics and Retail,** page 66). If you have the energy, climb the stairs to the top for the view over the city, and then come down and turn right along the **Via del Babuino**. In the distance you will see the **Obelisk of Piazza del Popolo (Romantics and Retail**, page 74, or **In the Footsteps of Caravaggio**, page 78), and beyond that the church of **S. Maria del Popolo**. If it is open, go in, as it is almost an art gallery, particularly famous for its two Caravaggios. This might be a moment to draw breath and have some refreshments in one of the two very expensive bars in this square, or in one of the cheaper ones in a neighbouring street.

Take the **Via Ripetta**, past the **Caffè Rosati**, to the end and keep going straight on, past the

S. Agnese in Piazza Navona.

Altar of Peace into the **Via della Scrofa**. Divert into the **Via di S. Agostino** on the right if you wish to see the Caravaggio in the church of **Sant' Agostino**, and into the church of **San Luigi** a bit further on for the same reason (there are three here), and then left down the **Via dei Giustiniani** into **Piazza della Rotonda** and **the Pantheon (Lost in the Folds of History**, page 86). Return up the Via dei Giustiniani, along the **Via del Salvatore**, across the **Corso Rinascimento** and into the **Piazza Navona**. Here is one of the most beautiful fountains in the city, the **Fountain of the Four Rivers**, and also a very handsome Baroque church, **S.Agnese (Lost in the Folds of History**, page 88).

At the bottom of the square to the left from where you entered it, go down the **Via della Cuccagna**, through the little **Piazza di S. Pantaleo**, across the busy **Corso Vittorio Emanuele** and up the **Via dei Baullari** into

the **Campo de' Fiori**. If it is a weekday morning, there will be a lively, colourful market, worth having a quick look round. The Via dei Baullari continues on the other side of the square and leads into the **Piazza Farnese**, dominated by the enormous and sublime **Palazzo Farnese** and with two of the most striking fountains of Rome, created out of enormous Roman granite bathtubs.

Off to the left take the **Via Capodiferro**, past the handsome **Palazzo Spada** (go into the courtyard and admire Borromini's *trompe-l'oeil* colonnade on the left), and at the end of the street turn right up the **Via dei Pettinari**. At the end of this, cross the Tiber on the **Ponte Sisto** (dating from the 1470s), and enter the **Piazza Trilussa** and **Trastevere (The Other Romans**, page 120). This area deserves several hours on its own, but given that you will almost certainly be flagging by now it is enough to walk through some of medieval streets to savour the atmosphere of this picturesque quarter and visit a couple of churches. With this in mind, leave the square by the **Via del Moro** on the left, following this to its end, turning right down the **Via della Lungaretta** and into the **Piazza di S. Maria in Trastevere**. On the far side is the very beautiful church of **S. Maria in Trastevere** (have a look at the 12thC mosaics inside), and round the square you will find bars and restaurants of one sort and another – a good point to stop for a snack, beer or cup of coffee while watching the fountain and children play. Taking the small street to the left from where you entered the square, pass through the **Piazza di S. Callisto** and into the long, straight **Via di S. Francesco a Ripa**, right down to the end and into the **Piazza di S. Francesco a Ripa**. Here turn left down the **Via Anicia**, following it as far as the first turning to the right, the **Via Madonna del Orto**. Take this and then turn left down the **Via di S. Michele** and into the **Piazza di S. Cecilia**, and through the gates into the glorious church of **Santa Cecilia** (peaceful courtyard and garden and 9thC mosaics). And now the last leg of this very long walk.

Turn left out of the church, on to the **Via di S. Cecilia** and then first left again, on to the **Via dei Genovesi**. Take the first right, down a fascinating, winding alley, **Vicolo dell'Atleta**, then left (**Via dei Salumi**) and second right into the **Piazza in Piscinula**. Over on the far side is a short flight of steps, which leads to a bridge to the **Tiber Island** (**Two Islands,** page 44). Glancing at the church of **S. Bartolomeo** to your right, take the bridge on the other side (**Ponte Fabricio** - it is Roman and dates from 62 BC). Keep to the right of the large cream-coloured Synagogue on the otherside of the river, turning left at the bottom, past the **Portico of Octavia**, left along the **Via del Portico d'Ottavia** down the second alley to the right, the **Via della Reginella**, into the **Piazza Mattei**, where you will see the **Fountain of the Tortoises**. The far side of this leads into the **Piazza Paganica**, which becomes the **Piazza dell'Enciclopedia Italiana**. At the end of this is the **Largo Argentina**, on the far side of which you will find a most welcome taxi rank.

Ponte Fabricio.

The Heart, Soul and Guts of Ancient Rome: The Capitol to the Cloaca Maxima

The main feature of this walk, the Capitoline Hill, has an interesting composite history – remnants from ancient Rome, the Middle Ages, the Renaissance, and the 19th and 20th centuries coexist and interlock, juxtaposed and superimposed. In classical times the hill was the most sacred spot of the city, as the great temple dedicated to the Capitoline Jupiter, or to the Capitoline Triad (Jupiter, Juno and Minerva), stood here from 509 BC. It was rebuilt several times, ever more splendidly, lastly by Domitian (81-96 AD) with gilded bronze tiles. The Forum was once the city's centre of gravity and the buildings on the hill faced towards it, but gradually the focus shifted to the Vatican and the commercial areas of the medieval city. In the 16th century Michelangelo designed the exquisite Piazza del

Campidoglio symbolically facing away from the Forum and towards the Vatican. Together with the superb buildings on three of its sides, the Piazza del Campidoglio is one of the glories of the modern city. This walk starts at the dazzlingly white Victor Emmanuel Monument tacked on to one slope of the hill, passes through Michelangelo's square, and then winds down the hill, round the edges of the Forum, peering into it at various points. It takes you past some of the most ancient and attractive churches in the city, and the two oldest temples still standing, ending up where the great sewer of ancient Rome empties into the Tiber.

Statue of Marcus Aurelius.

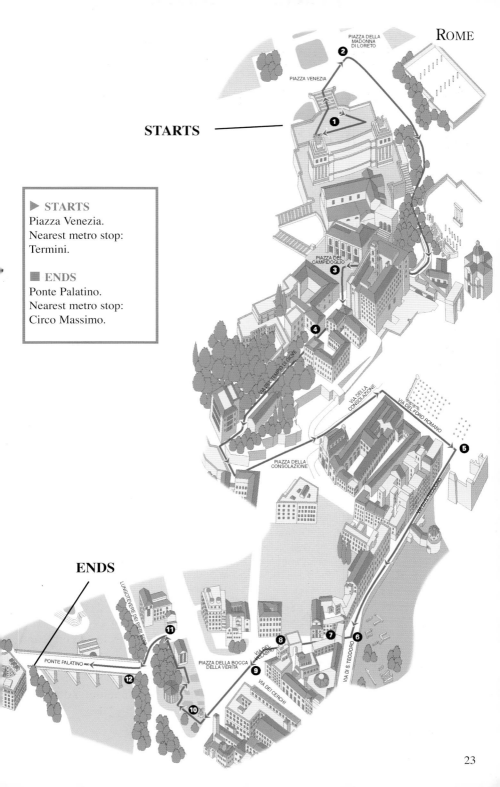

ROME

STARTS ——————

STARTS
Piazza Venezia.
Nearest metro stop:
Termini.

ENDS
Ponte Palatino.
Nearest metro stop:
Circo Massimo.

PIAZZA DELLA
MADONNA
DI LORETO

PIAZZA VENEZIA

PIAZZA DEL
CAMPIDOGLIO

VIA DEL TEMPIO DI GIOVE

VIA DELLA
CONSOLAZIONE

VIA DEL FORO ROMANO

PIAZZA DELLA
CONSOLAZIONE

ENDS ——————

LUNGOTEVERE DEI PIERLEONI

PONTE PALATINO

PIAZZA DELLA BOCCA
DELLA VERITA

VIA DI S. TEODORO

VIA DEI CERCHI

23

❶ The enormous white mass of the **Victor Emmanuel Monument** has roused strong and contrasting emotions ever since its construction, which began in 1885 and lasted some 45 years. It was built to celebrate Italy's reemergence as a single nation and serves as a general declaration of national pride. After the collapse of the Roman Empire, Italy had been divided into various states whose boundaries varied over the centuries, and it wasn't until 1870 that Rome became the capital of the country, after a long process of reunification lasting some 31 years. Rome became capital under King Victor Emmanuel II, who gave his name to the monument. With its glaring whiteness, lofty columns and long flights of steps, all in shining marble, topped by bronze chariots and horses, it lords it over the centre of the city. This is after all, albeit in an exaggerated form, what much of ancient Rome looked like. Climb as high as possible in the building for the view from its various terraces, or for a hefty sum take the lift at the back up to the very top for an unrivalled panorama over the city.

❷ Back down at ground level, bear right and take the steep **Via S. Pietro in Carcere** or the even steeper steps, the **Scala dell'Arce Capitolina**, leading up to the **Capitoline Square (Campidoglio)** at the top, designed by Michelangelo and of an extraordinary harmony and refinement. Just before entering the square, the steps continue to the right, leading to one of Rome's most beautiful medieval churches, **S. Maria in Aracoeli**, huge and unusually light for its period, dating to the end of the 13th century. Admire the wonderful gilded and coffered ceiling, the Bufalini chapel frescoed by Pinturicchio (last on the left) and the adorable idol of the baby Jesus, credited with extraordinary miraculous powers. Go out at the far end and on to the terrace to see the church's sobre brick façade, the precipitous 124 steps which are the official

way up to the sanctuary, and another fine panorama.

❸ Return through the church and find your way back to the **Piazza del Campidoglio**. Facing each other across the square are the elegant palaces housing the Capitoline Museums – the oldest public collection in the world and one of the city's most interesting mixed collections. View such treasures as *The Capitoline Wolf* (Etruscan bronze), *The Boy Pulling out a Thorn* (Hellenistic bronze), *The Dying Gaul* (marble), the colossal marble head of Constantine, as well as fine pictures, porcelain, Roman micromosaics, busts, the great platform on which stood the temple of Capitoline Jupiter, and so on. To the back of the square is the most handsome town hall anywhere, the Palazzo Senatorio, which houses Rome's city council and the mayor's offices. In the middle stands the striking bronze statue of Marcus Aurelius (actually, this is a copy – the original is now under cover in the museum). This is a very rare survival as most Roman bronze statues, of which there were many hundreds throughout the city, were at some point melted down. Marcus Aurelius was spared this fate because he was long wrongly believed to be Constantine, the friend of the Christians.

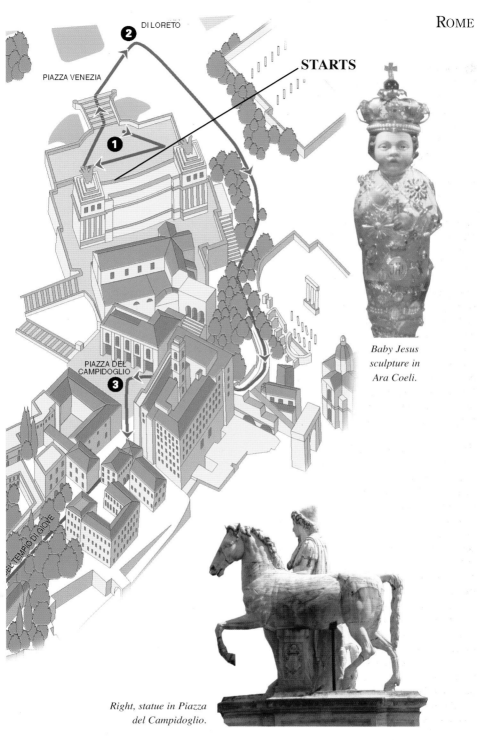

DI LORETO

PIAZZA VENEZIA

STARTS

PIAZZA DEL CAMPIDOGLIO

DEL TEMPIO DI GIOVE

Baby Jesus sculpture in Ara Coeli.

Right, statue in Piazza del Campidoglio.

❹ Taking the flight of steps which lead up to the right of the **Palazzo Senatorio**, through the building at the top, you will emerge in the **Via Tempio di Giove**. If this way is barred, take the **Via del Campidoglio** leading towards the Forum and turn right up the **Via Monte Tarpeo** (from here there is a spectacular view over the Forum, with the Colosseum in the background) and then right again at the end, to join the Via Tempio di Giove. To the right were the precincts of the temple. Head straight on to the end, next to the sign saying 'Via di Villa Caffarelli', through a gate and down some steps. There are various terraces and paths on the hill at this point, but make your way to the bottom and turn left up the **Vico Jugario**, as far as the square with a big church on the far side, **S. Maria della Consolazione**. Lovers of wrought iron should enter, as there are two very fine sets of 16th/17thC gates (the third chapel on right and left), but otherwise continue straight on as far as the Forum and the **Via Foro Romano**. Tantalizingly, there are views but no access on this side – follow the road to the end and turn right down the **Via S. Teodoro**.

❺ This takes its name from the church of **S.**

Teodoro, attractively set in a courtyard down steps and in part very ancient (5thC rebuilt in 15th), but internally rather disappointing and devoid of interest.

❻ Further on to the right, take the **Via del Velabro**, and you will soon come to the enchanting church of **S. Giorgio al Velabro**, also of considerable antiquity (9thC, with additions), porticoed and with a handsome Romanesque belltower. On entering through the fine recycled classical frame, you will find a peaceful interior, the aisle lined with columns in a mixture of styles, some of fluted marble, others of granite, and a mixture of capitals. The altar is of Cosmatesque mosaic work.

❼ Coming out and turning right you will come upon a strange little arch attached to the church, the **Arco degli Argentarii**, erected in AD 204 by the guild of money changers (the meaning of Argentarii) and dedicated to the emperor Septimius Severus and his wife, Julia Domna, and their sons, Geta and Caracalla. There are portraits of three of them, the emperor and his wife on the right inside face, and Caracalla on the left (Geta was murdered by his brother and his portrait erased).

S. Giorgio al Velabro.

S.Teodoro.

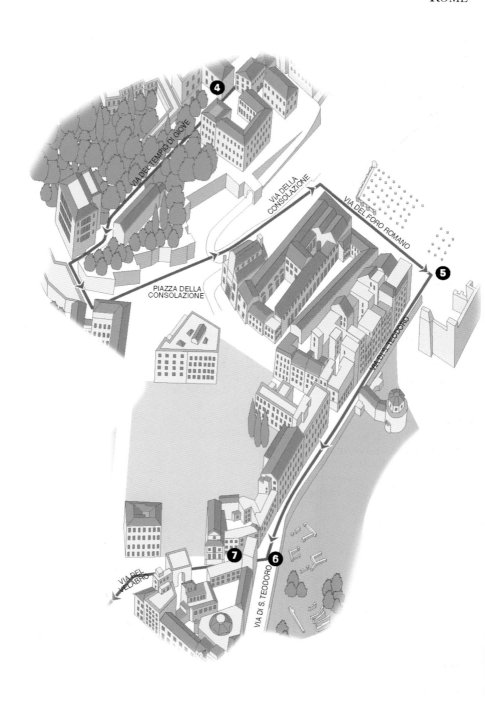

VIA DEL TEMPIO DI GIOVE

VIA DELLA CONSOLAZIONE

VIA DEL FORO ROMANO

PIAZZA DELLA CONSOLAZIONE

VIA DI S. TEODORO

VIA DEL VELABRO

VIA DI S. TEODORO

Temple dedicated to Hercules the Victor.

Temple of Portumnus.

8 In the space beyond this monument is a severe, square structure, a quadruple arch, known as the **Arch of Janus**. This probably dates to the 4th century and perhaps served as entrance to the livestock market of Rome, the Forum Boarium, which occupied much of this area of the ancient city.

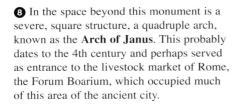

Left, the Bocca Della Verità in S. Maria in Cosmedin.

9 Beyond, you come to a rather shapeless open area, the **Piazza della Bocca della Verità**, with traffic hurtling from all directions. On the left rises the 8thC church of **S. Maria in Cosmedin**, with its slightly later belltower. The interior has interesting examples of ancient stonework, floors, bishop's chair and so on, but the most famous feature of the church is the **Bocca della Verità**, or 'Mouth of Truth', originally a Roman draincover, fashioned like a rather sinister face. This now stands in the portico and according to legend, bites off the fingers of those who tell a lie while holding their fingers in its mouth. It has an abiding fascination for tourists and features in every guide book, so there is usually a long queue of all nationalities, waiting to be photographed with their hand in its mouth.

10 Across the road is a pretty Berniniesque **fountain of tritons** (by Bizzaccheri, 1715),

PIAZZA DELLA BOCCA DELLA VERITA

and beyond that a pair of small temples, one round and one rectangular, the oldest standing monuments in the city. The round one, drawn, sketched, painted and printed innumerable times and often known erroneously as the Temple of Vesta, is in fact to Hercules the Victor and dates to the end of the 2nd century BC. The rectangular one, once thought to be of Fortuna Virile, is in fact of the river god, Portumnus, and is possibly very slightly later. Now surrounded by oleanders and greenery, they form an attractive oasis amidst the swirling traffic.

The Arch of Janus, the only quadrifons triumphal arch still standing in Rome.

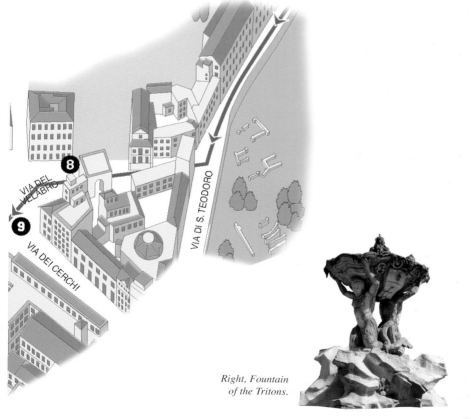

Right, Fountain of the Tritons.

⓫ To the far side of the piazza is a strange house, much restored, and constructed largely of classical fragments, known as the **house of the Crescenzi** (a prominent medieval Roman family). This house probably dates to the middle of the 11th century. Up the slope to the left you will come to the road which runs along the river embankment. It is not at all easy to cross at this point, but if you eventually manage to, head for the bridge, the **Ponte Palatino**, on which the traffic seems to flow in the English way, on the left. To the right is the remaining arch of a ruined bridge, covered in caper plants, known as the **Ponte Rotto** (the Broken Bridge). The first masonry bridge of ancient Rome was built here (181-179 BC), but the river becomes particularly turbulent during floods, with the result that bridges on this site were washed away and rebuilt numerous times. This last happened in the 16th century, when Michelangelo and the other architects attempted a restoration, only to have their efforts completely destroyed in the disastrous floods of 1598. It was then abandoned.

The rather neglected Cloaca Maxima.

⓬ There is a flight of steps down to the river on the right of this bridge. Having descended to river level, walk along the embankment under the bridge. Almost immediately you will come to the mouth of the **Cloaca Maxima**, the great sewer dating back to the 6th century BC and continuously in use from then on. A trickle of dirty water flows out of it to this day, but it is now a melancholy spot, neglected and overgrown with fig trees.

Interesting architecture of Casa dei Crescenzi.

Ponte Rotte, the ruins of the 2ndC masonry bridge, abandoned in the 16th century.

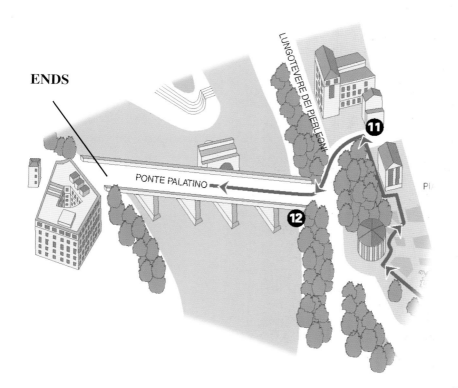

ENDS

PONTE PALATINO

LUNGOTEVERE DEI PIERLEONI

Living Archaeology: The Forum, the Palatine and the Caelian Hill

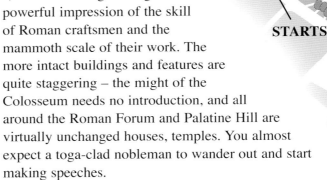

Trajan's Column is a jaw-dropping work of art, and an apt starting point for a walk that explores the genius of Roman design. Although a lot of what you will see on the walk is in ruins, even these fragments give a powerful impression of the skill of Roman craftsmen and the mammoth scale of their work. The more intact buildings and features are quite staggering – the might of the Colosseum needs no introduction, and all around the Roman Forum and Palatine Hill are virtually unchanged houses, temples. You almost expect a toga-clad nobleman to wander out and start making speeches.

It's the Rome of history books – here Romulus founded the city after murdering his brother Remus, there Marc Antony made his famous speech following the death of Julius Caesar. If you're travelling with kids, this is a walk for them – they can roam free round the Palatine and Forum and experience the ruins literally 'hands on'. For the adults, it's an exhilarating and sobering experience all in one – the fall of a mighty civilisation brought vividly to life.

Trajan's Column.

Arch of Constantine.

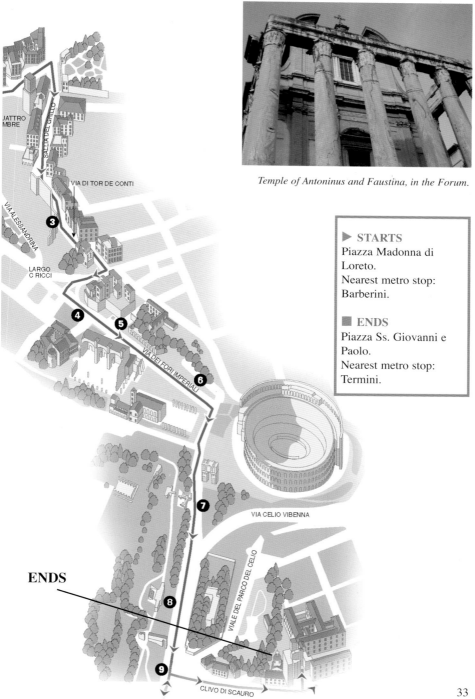

Temple of Antoninus and Faustina, in the Forum.

▶ **STARTS**
Piazza Madonna di
Loreto.
Nearest metro stop:
Barberini.

■ **ENDS**
Piazza Ss. Giovanni e
Paolo.
Nearest metro stop:
Termini.

QUATTRO
MBRE

SALITA DEL GRILLO

VIA DI TOR DE CONTI

VIA ALESSANDRINA

3

LARGO
C RICCI

4

5

VIA DEI FORI IMPERIALI

6

7

VIA CELIO VIBENNA

VIALE DEL PARCO DEL CELIO

ENDS

8

9

CLIVO DI SCAURO

33

Trajan's Market.

❶ **Trajan's Forum** was the last and grandest of the Imperial Fora, built with the spoils of Trajan's Dacian wars in the early 110s AD. The citizens of the city had long outgrown the Roman Forum, the traditional hub of public life, and this was Trajan's solution to the need for more space. Constructed from coloured, polished marble with bronze and gold embellishments, it must have been an astonishing sight. The ruins that remain can hardly do it justice, but the column is still remarkable – around 2,500 carved figures spiral up the 40 m

Church Santissimo Node di Maria, behind Trajan's Column.

length, providing a highly unusual but accurate account of the Dacian campaigns. The 18 marble blocks were originally coloured and crowned by a statue of Trajan – the current figure of St Peter only took his place in 1587. The Emperor's ashes lie in the chamber at the bottom. The huge, red brick complex to the side is **Trajan's Market**, a strikingly intact and evocative reminder of everyday life in ancient times.

❷ Head up the steps opposite the column (**Via Magnanapoli**) and on to the **Via Quatre Novembre**. Keep going uphill, past the Museum of the Imperial Fora on your right, and turn right at the cross roads, with gorgeous Angelicum church on your left. Go through **Largo Angelicum** on to **Salita del Grillo** and see the faded grandeur of **Piazza del Grillo**. Continue straight ahead as it becomes **Tor del Conti**, looking to your right for a sudden, secret view into Trajan's Market – there won't be any tourists here. The toppled pillars are enormous, and give some idea of the original scale of Trajan's projects.

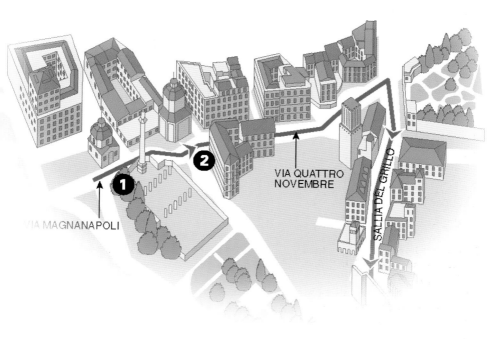

VIA QUATTRO
NOVEMBRE

SALLIA DEL GRILLO

VIA MAGNANAPOLI

Below, the back of Trajan's
Market, from Sal del Grillo.
Below left, wall detail on
Tor del Conti.

❸ Continue onwards on Tor del Conti, which opens on to **Largo Corrado Ricci**. Turn right and keep ahead to the railings overlooking the **Roman Forum** – you won't be able to miss them, there'll be a knot of tourists jostling for elbow room and a steady stream heading for the entrance to the left. If you manage to find some space, feast your eyes on the spectacle below – the half-standing, half-toppled remains of the city's great meeting place. At once commercial, ceremonial and political, the Forum grew up in the hollow between four of Rome's hills. The ruins span some 1,000 years of construction, layer upon layer, offering a glimpse into the realities of Roman public life. The crowds of sightseers are probably modest compared with the crowds of Roman citizens, who gathered here to pray, eat, conduct business, play sport and attend the courts, where great orators such as Cicero held sway.

❹ If you've made it all the way to Rome, you really may as well spend the 12 euros (as this guide went to press) on the combined ticket for the Forum, Palatine and Colosseum. However, unless you are particularly keen to see the Forum right away, it is worth bypassing the queues here and at the Colosseum, and buying your entrance ticket at the quieter Palatine, half a mile onwards. From the Palatine you can wander back into the Forum, and the walk ends only a short distance from the Colosseum. You'll get a useful map with your ticket, which notes all the main sites of interest, though if you're really keen it's worth arming yourself with a more detailed guide.

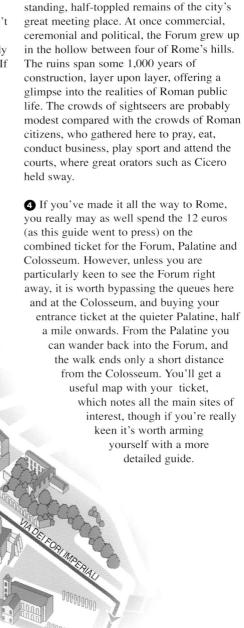

To be honest, though, it's most fun to simply wander where your feet take you. The ruins are oddly moving, despite the crowds, and the mighty scale offers a unique perspective on things. It's a place in which to get philosophical.

❺ Assuming you will want to skip the queues and use the Palatine entrance, our route continues towards the **Colosseum**, left if you are standing with the Forum in front of you. Don't cross the road, because soon, on your right, you'll see the rather unprepossessing exterior of the **SS Cosma e Damiano**, built in a hall of Vespasian's Forum of Peace. Do resist the temptation to power on to the Colosseum and go inside, because a lovely serene, sunny courtyard leads on to a spectacularly decorated church. Check out the quite modern-looking mosaic over the apse, with a charming row of sheep below – it's actually 6thC, in the Byzantine style. A huge glass window at the back looks down on to the 3rdC BC Temple of Jupiter Stator.

Top, ornate ruins in the Palatine. Above left, a beautifully sculpted column in Largo Corrado Ricci and above right, a plaque in the courtyard of SS Cosma e Damiano.

View of the Forum.

The Colosseum.

6 Continue towards the Colosseum with the remains of the Forum of Peace on your right-hand side and the 'story' of the Roman Forum on your left (free entrance – a pleasant place to sit and rest a while with a drink or ice cream). As you get closer to the Colosseum, you will see an enormous arch to the right – head towards it, looking into the Forum complex on your right for a fine view of the **Arch of Titus**, built in AD 81 to celebrate the destruction of Jerusalem. In front of you is the **Arch of Constantine**, the largest and best preserved of Rome's triumphal arches. It was dedicated to the Emperor in 315 after his victory over the usurping Emperor Maxentius at Ponte Milvio. Note the inscription instinctu divinitatis ('by the will of the divinity') on the dedication above the main arch – though veiled, it's the first official reference on the face of Imperial Rome to the newly adopted Christian God.

7 Go past the Arch of Constantine, keep straight on and you will come to the **Palatine** entrance on your right, where the queues for the combined tickets are much shorter. The rise and fall of Classical Rome is written in the stones of the **Palatine Hill** – from the cave where Romulus and Remus were famously succoured by the she-wolf, to the bloated palaces of its emperors, each

built to eclipse the others, so that the Hill is now a honeycomb of ruins. People have lived in the site since approximately 1000 BC, and in Roman mythology it is where Romulus decided to found his eponymous city, after murdering his brother. Despite its august history, the Palatine is a peaceful spot – birds sing, wild flowers abound, and the whole place is surprisingly fragrant. You can certainly see why it became the place to live for emperors and wealthy Romans. The sheer scale of it means that the crowds are absorbed and you can wander in relative solitude around the half-mighty, half-crumbling buildings. Plus it's delightfully health-and-safety free – no roped-off areas. If you only see one thing, make it **Domitian's stadium,** so intact you hardly need to imagine the way it once looked, filled with Roman sportsmen.

Entrance to the Palatine.

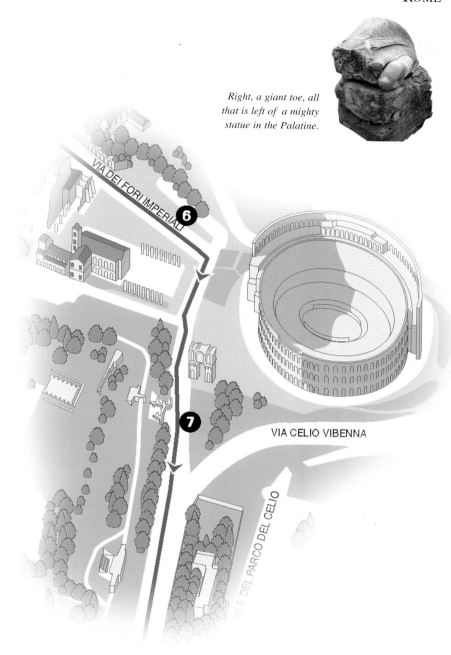

Right, a giant toe, all that is left of a mighty statue in the Palatine.

VIA DEI FORI IMPERIALI

6

7

VIA CELIO VIBENNA

VIALE DEL PARCO DEL CELIO

❽ Coming out of the Palatine entrance, turn right and continue along **Via di San Gregorio**. It's pretty noisy and dusty, but it's not long until you reach the famous **Circus Maximus** (not shown on map). A sad shadow of its former glory – it was the first and largest chariot stadium in Rome – yet the sheer size of it, the still-visible spina or central island, and the remains of a seating platform, still make for an impressive sight. It once held up to 300,000 spectators, roughly a quarter of the population of Rome.

❾ With your back to the Circus, facing the road you came from, turn right (you want the red brick two-storey building surrounded by steps on your left). There's a road just beyond this building with steps leading upwards – don't take these, but follow the road round to the left, and you'll very soon come to the **Monastero di San Gregorio Magno** on your right (not shown on map). Keep going, and the road turns into **Clivo di Scauro**. Turn right uphill on this road,

until you reach **Case Romane del Celio** on your left (open 10am-1pm/3pm-6pm every day, except Tuesday and Wednesday). After the grandeur of the Forum and the Palatine, the Case Romane offers a snapshot of domestic Roman life. Excavations on the site revealed more than 20 rooms, some beautifully decorated, dating from 4th-13thC AD. The paintings are exquisite, and on a pleasingly manageable scale after the gargantuan ruins of earlier. Entrance cost €6 as this guide went to press.

❿ Next visit **Santi Giovanni e Paolo** on your left. The interior is certainly eye-catching, with dozens of ornate glass chandeliers and frilly white pedestals lining the aisles – it comes as no surprise to learn that it's a popular wedding venue. The door next to the gorgeous red brick tower leads into a cool, dark space looking down on to giant ancient foundations – necessary, given the gigantic scale on which the Romans built. Come out again, and to your left are the pretty white gates of **Villa Celimontana**, which leads into **Celio Park**, a grassy expanse laced with cool paths. It's blissfully quiet – more of a local park for jogging and lunch breaks than a tourist spot. There are often donkey rides for the kids and a useful public toilet. To get back to the Colosseum (where there is a metro stop), turn right out of the white gates up the **Via S.Paolo della Croce** and at the end turn left down the **Via Claudia**. The Colosseum will soon loom into view up ahead.

Tower of Giovanna e Paolo.

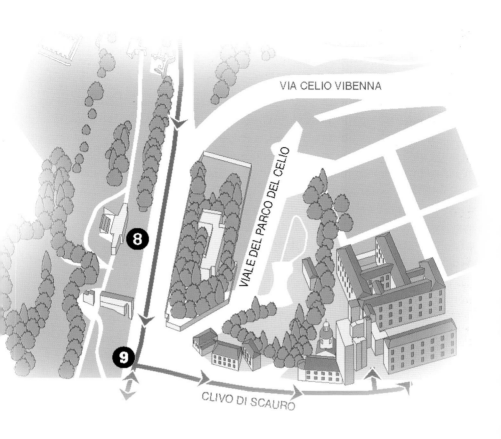

VIA CELIO VIBENNA

VIALE DEL PARCO DEL CELIO

CLIVO DI SCAURO

*Statue of Mother Teresa
outside San Gregorio
Magno.*

Celio Park.

Two Islands: The Isola Tiberina and the Jewish Ghetto

This winding walk curves around the area at the foot of the Capitoline Hill, one of the most important monumental quarters of the ancient city, much of which was built by Emperor Augustus (28BC-14AD) in honour of various members of his family. He boasted that he had inherited a city in brick and left one in marble, and this was one of the parts of Rome on which he concentrated his efforts. In medieval times it was filled with narrow residential streets and picturesque squares, many of which still survive, and in the following centuries grand palaces and churches grew up all round the edges. Here is also to be found the Jewish Ghetto, a very low-lying area beside the river, notoriously prone to flooding. In 1555, Pope Paul IV (1555-1559) built a wall around the quarter, with three gates that were locked at night. This established segregation and a long period of Jewish persecution. Reputedly a harsh man, the Pope was much hated by the Roman populace and his statue can be seen in the church of S. Maria

sopra Minerva ('Life at the Top' walk, pages 92-99). The itinerary meanders along narrow medieval and Renaissance streets, through modest but beautiful piazzas, past one of Rome's greatest churches and an exquisite fountain, covering a chronological range from the 1st century BC to the early 20th century. At many points there are excellent restaurants – especially in the ghetto where you can try Roman Jewish specialities, including delicious deep-fried artichokes.

Temple of Apollo, above, and Theatre of Marcellus, right.

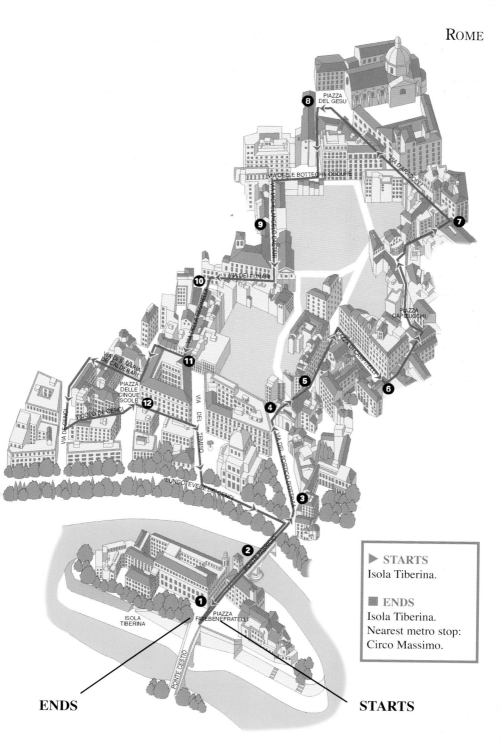

PIAZZA
DEL GESU

8

VIA D'ARACOELI

7

VIA DELLE BOTTEGHE OSCURE

VIA MICHELANGELO CAETANI

9

VIA DEI FUNARI

10

PIAZZA
CAPIZUCCHI

VIA DELLA REGINELLA

VIA DEI CALDERARI

PIAZZA DI CAMPITELLI

11

VIA DI S. MARIA
DE' CALDERARI

5

PIAZZA
DELLE
CINQUE
SCOLE

12

6

VICOLO DE' CENCI

VIA DE' CENCI

VIA DEL TEMPIO

4

VIA DEL PORTICO D'OTTAVIA

3

LUNGOTEVERE DE' CENCI

2

PONTE FABRICIO

1

ISOLA
TIBERINA

PIAZZA
FATEBENEFRATELLI

PONTE CESTIO

ENDS

STARTS

▶ **STARTS**
Isola Tiberina.

■ **ENDS**
Isola Tiberina.
Nearest metro stop:
Circo Massimo.

43

Two Islands: The Isola Tiberina and the Jewish Ghetto

Portico of Octavia.

① The **Tiber Island**, which divides the river into two branches, has been associated with healing since at least the 3rd century BC, when a temple to the Greek god of medicine, Aesculapius, was built there. A direct descendant of this tradition is St Bart's, the London teaching hospital, founded in 1123 by Henry I's courtier, Rahere, who was cured here having fallen ill while on pilgrimage in Rome. He had a vision and founded the hospital to commemorate his recovery, naming the new foundation after St Bartholomew, whose church bounds one side of the attractive square, the **Piazza S. Bartolomeo**. What little remained of the apostle after he had been skinned alive by the Romans is preserved in the church, which is handsome but does not contain much of interest.

② With your back to Trastevere, cross over the ancient bridge, the **Ponte Fabricio** (Pons Fabricius), which dates to 62 BC and remains largely intact. If you wish to observe the bridge properly, take the flight of steps on the right at the end, which lead down to the river embankment.

③ Across the road at the traffic lights is the **Jewish Ghetto**, to which you will be returning at the end of the itinerary. To your right you'll pass a chapel with inscriptions in Latin and Hebrew. This was one of the several sites of Christian worship in which members of the Jewish community were forced to attend Catholic services, in an attempt to convert them to the 'true' religion. Skirting the imposing synagogue to your left, and glancing at the inscription on the wall on your right, memorializing the deportations of Jews and others to Nazi concentration camps, head for the columns ahead, which rise from a level below the modern street. This is the **Portico of Octavia**, built by Augustus 27–23 BC and named after his sister. What you see today are the remains of the entrance to a rectangular, monumental enclosure in which were to be found two small temples (look for the helpful illustration down in the excavations). If you have time, go down into these excavations and walk round to have a close look at the **Theatre of Marcellus**, but if a distant view is enough, continue as directed below.

④ Squeeze past the well-known restaurant to the left, **Da Giggetto**, known for its Roman Jewish specialities, along the passage to the side of the monument, and bear right along the **Via della Tribuna di Campitelli**. Take the sharp corner to the right, which brings you to a vantage point overlooking the three columns of the **Temple of Apollo Sosianus** and the Theatre of Marcellus. Completed by Augustus in about 11 BC and dedicated to his nephew and son-in-law, the theatre once seated up to 15,000 spectators and inspired the architecture of the Colosseum, which was begun some 80 years later. After Rome's collapse, the monument was treated as a quarry and much of the cut stone from it was removed to be recycled elsewhere. However, in the middle of the 16th century what was left of the monument was taken over by the Savelli family, who built the palace you see today at the top. This palace is still in private hands and reportedly the most expensive private accommodation in the city.

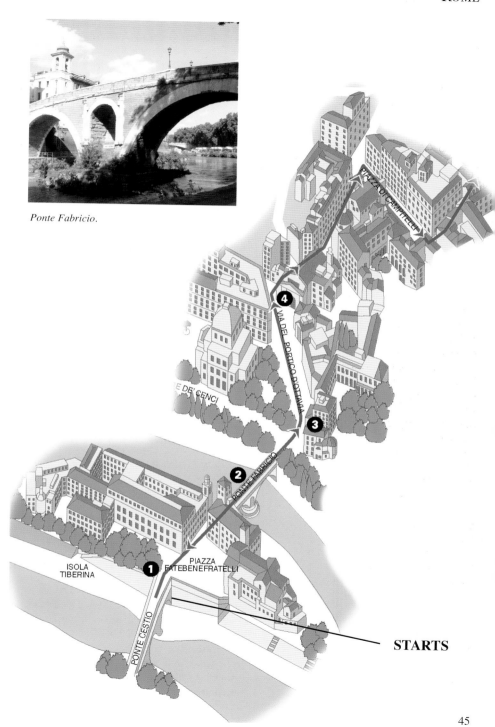

Ponte Fabricio.

PIAZZA DI CAMPITELLI

4

VIA DEL PORTICO D'OTTAVIA

E DE' CENCI

3

2

PONTE FABRICIO

ISOLA
TIBERINA

1

PIAZZA
FATEBENEFRATELLI

PONTE CESTIO

STARTS

5 On up the Via della Tribuna di Campitelli, past the row of fine and ancient columns built into the wall of **no. 23**, and round to the right into the **Piazza Campitelli**. You will then pass on the corner one of Rome's best old-fashioned, elegant restaurants, **La Vecchia Roma** (Piazza Campitelli 18). Go into the splendid church next to it, **S. Maria in Campitelli** – a quick glance is enough to admire the sumptuous, gilded creation over the altar, the *raggiera*, designed to hold the sacred icon of the Madonna, and the polychrome marbles of several of the side-chapels. In a side chapel on the left, there is also a somewhat Disneyesque glass casket in which the mortal remains of 16thC S. Giovanni Leopardi are displayed.

6 At the end of the square turn left down the narrow and twisting **Via Capizucchi**, through the **Piazza Capizucchi**, into the enchanting **Piazza Margana** (where you'll

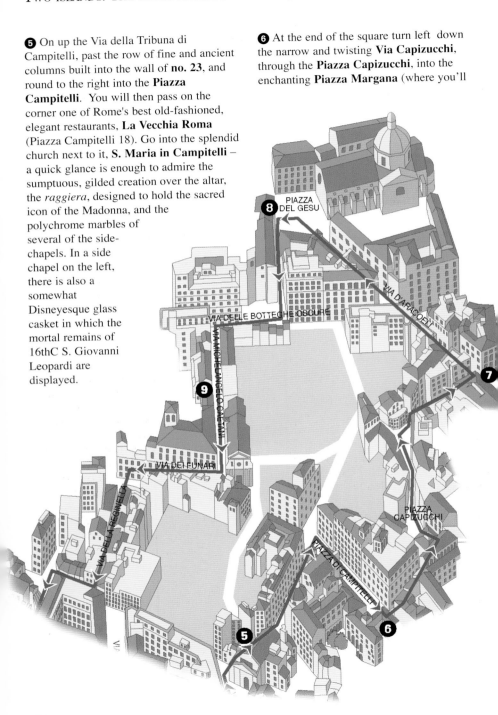

46

Casket of S. Giovanni Leopardi in S. Maria in Campitelli.

find another excellent restaurant, the **Taverna degli Amici**). Look up at the tower decorated with Roman architectural bits and pieces (**no 40 and 40a**) and the doorway of **no 32**, down the **Via Margana**, to the end where you turn left.

❼ Now down the **Via di Aracoeli** to the square at the end, the **Piazza del Gesù**, dominated by the great, mainly 16thC **Chiesa del Gesù**, in which the founder of the Jesuit order, St Ignatius of Loyola is buried. Before entering, look at the rather dramatic statues of the saint on the façade, one with his foot on the neck of a female heathen, pointing sternly at a passage in the Bible, and the other with his foot on the neck of a male heathen, brandishing a whip. Once inside, admire the frescoes of the main vault, *Triumph of the Name of Jesus* (1679), by Baciccia, a wonderful *trompe-l'oeil* riot, with shadows, clouds and figures tumbling out of the frame and down the vault. Then head for the extraordinarily richly decorated chapel on the left of the church which houses the great saint's tomb – rarely will you have seen so much *lapis lazuli* and gilt. At 5.30 pm every day of the year (except during Lent) the chapel provides some of the best free entertainment to be found in the city. Heavenly choir music strikes up, interspersed with readings detailing the saint's dying days. In a spectacular climax, the church lights turn on as the picture over the altar slides down to reveal a massive silver statue of St Ignatius reaching ecstatically up towards heaven.

❽ Once out of the church, head left and up the narrow **Via Celsa**, turn right along the **Via delle Botteghe Oscure**, and, if interested in the history of early medieval and Byzantine Rome, make a quick visit to the **Museo Nazionale Romano della Crypta di Balbo** on the far side of the street, before turning left up the **Via M. Caetani**. Here the body of Aldo Moro (former leader of the Italian Christian Democrat party and several times Prime Minister), was found murdered by the terrorist Red Brigades in May 1978. His car was intercepted on 16th March in a Rome suburb; in the course of the bloody gun battle that ensued, five members of his entourage were killed and he was kidnapped. He was then held captive for 54 days, in spite of hundreds of police raids, before being shot through the head and dumped here in the boot of a Renault 4 on 9th May.

❾ Opposite the memorial to this gruesome incident, go up a flight of steps and into the courtyard of the 17thC **Palazzo Mattei di Giove**, whose walls are lined with a spectacular range of Roman statuary and sarcophagi, and continue up the stairs to see some of the finest pieces. This is also a rare opportunity to wander freely round a great Roman palace without being challenged by a watchful porter.

Left, statue of Saint Ignatius.

10 Out through the other door of the palace, turn right and you will almost immediately be aware of the gentle splash of water, and just around the corner you'll come upon the **Fountain of the Tortoises**. The most charming of Rome's small fountains, it dates to the 1580s (the tortoises were added by Bernini in 1658). Then head down the **Via della Reginella** on one side of the little **Piazza Mattei**, and back into the Ghetto.

11 Here turn right into the **Via del Portico d'Ottavia**. On the corner at **no. 1** is an unpretentious Jewish *pasticceria* that is much more of an institution in Rome than it would appear. It sells a limited range of cakes and pastries that are renowned throughout the city, the most famous being the exquisite ricotta and morello cherry tart. And then left into the **Piazza Cinque Scole**, right along the **Via di S. Maria dei Calderari**, past the famous **Ristorante Il Pompiere**. Turn almost immediately left, pass under the dark and sinister arch, the **Arco de' Cenci**, and then left again up the steep and picturesque **Via Monte de' Cenci**, passing the best-known restaurant in the area **Piperno**, where the very finest *carciofi alla giudìa*, deep-fried artichokes in the Jewish style, are reputed to be served.

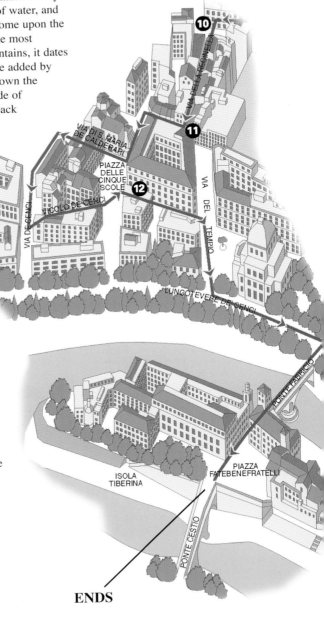

ENDS

Palazzo Mattei staircase.   *Palazzo Mattei staircase.*

⓬ Straight ahead is the **Via Catalana**, at the end of which stands the imposing synagogue, dating to 1904 and supposedly of Babylonian inspiration. On the river side is the entrance to the small and thought-provoking **Museo Ebraico**, the Jewish Museum. Here you will find silver ritual vessels, Torah scroll holders and poignant receipts for gold gathered together in attempts to ransom family members held during the Nazi occupation of Rome.

Fountain of the Tortoises.   *Palazzo Mattei statue.*

Baroque Splendour: Grand Piazzas, Backstreets, and Diocletian's Baths

This walk offers a fine introduction to the layering effect of (relatively) new Rome on to old Rome, which is in evidence all over the city. New foundations are laid over old; new buildings inhabit and adapt ancient ones; new structures plunder ruins for marble, stone and decorative features. For 'new', read 'a mere few centuries ago' – most of this walk focuses on 16th-18thC buildings, many in the Baroque style characterised by bold, emotional themes and dramatic contours. Love or hate Baroque (and plenty do hate it), you have to admit that its unabashed extravagance demands the viewer's full attention. In many cases, the layering of new on old is highly significant. Where churches inhabit old pagan institutions, it is often a symbolic victory for Christianity – thus Pope Pius IV's Santa Maria degli Angeli, in the Piazza della Repubblica, and Pope Clement XI's meridian line inside it (see points ❽ and ❾), which celebrates the Gregorian reform of the pagan Julian calendar. For real living, breathing history, time your visit to the Piazza del Quirinale for the changing of the guard (see point ❷). The two sentries who guard the presidential palace are exchanged in a fabulously intricate traditional routine – the rhythm and precision of their movements is quite hypnotic, and the whole experience is a fitting start to a walk full of grandeur.

> ► STARTS
> Piazza del Quirinale.
> Nearest metro stop:
> Barberini.

Palazzo del Quirinale

Giardini del Quirinale

PIAZZA DEL QUIRINALE

STARTS

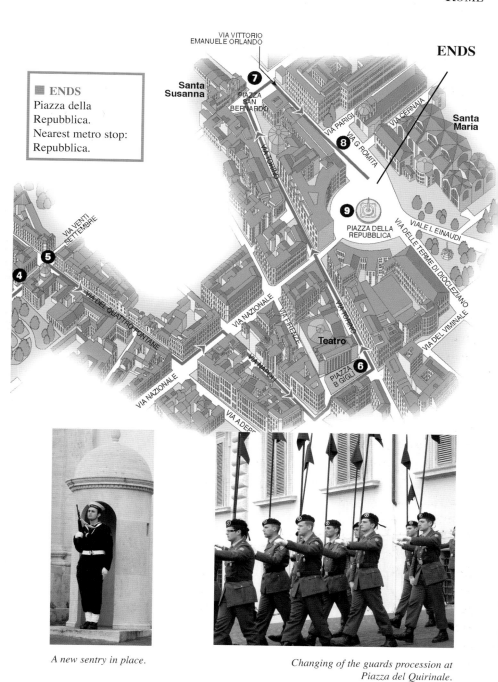

ENDS
Piazza della
Repubblica.
Nearest metro stop:
Repubblica.

VIA VITTORIO
EMANUELE ORLANDO

ENDS

Santa
Susanna

PIAZZA
SAN
BERNARDO

Santa
Maria

VIA PARIGI

VIA CERNAIA

VIA G. ROMITA

VIA TORINO

PIAZZA DELLA
REPUBBLICA

VIALE L EINAUDI

VIA DELLE TERME DI DIOCLEZIANO

VIA VENTI
SETTEMBRE

VIA DEL QUATTRO FONTANE

VIA NAZIONALE

VIA FIRENZE

Teatro

VIA TORINO

VIA DEL VIMINALE

VIA NAZIONALE

VIA NAPOLI

PIAZZA
B GIGLI

VIA A DEPR

A new sentry in place.

*Changing of the guards procession at
Piazza del Quirinale.*

51

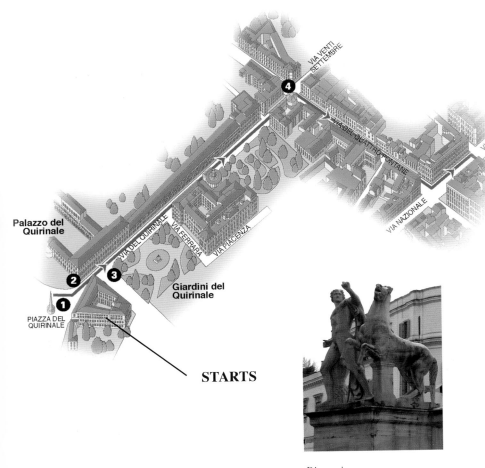

Dioscuri.

❶ The **Piazza del Quirinale** is one of Rome's most
beautiful squares. Its centrepiece is the splendid
Dioscuri fountain, a real hybrid of treasures – the colossal statues of the two horse-tamers
Castor and Pollux came from the nearby Baths of Constantine; the obelisk is from the
Mausoleum of Augustus; the granite bowl of the fountain once lay in the Roman Forum,
used as a cattle trough.

❷ The **Palazzo del Quirinale**, Gregory XIII's 16thC Papal summer residence, is now the
official home of Italy's presidents. It's well worth coinciding with the changing of the guards
at 3.15pm (4pm on holidays) – these ritualistic, almost balletic movements are a sight to
behold. Army and Navy troops emerge from both sides of the courtyard and meet in the
middle for the National Anthem (complete with marching band), and the exchange of
sentries. To the west of the square is a balcony view of Rome and opposite the Quirinale is
the 18thC **Palazzo della Consulta**, Italy's Constitutional Court, with a façade by Fuga.

Above, one of the Quattro Fontane. Right, Outside Sant'Andrea.

King Carlo Alberto statue.

Above, one of the Quattro Fontane.

❸ With your back to the fountain, walk straight ahead on to the **Via del Quirinale**, passing pocket-handkerchief **Giardini del Quirinale** on your right, presided over by the heroic equestrian statue of King Carlo Alberto, father of United Italy's first monarch. **Sant'Andrea al Quirinale**, the little oval-domed church on your right, was designed by Bernini, and the often self-critical artist thought it one of his finest works. Even die-hard critics of Baroque will find it hard not to be swept up in this *tour de force* of gilt and marble, with its fabulously ornate altar-piece and unsettling life-size crucifix.

❹ Keep going in the same direction until you meet **Via delle Quattro Fontane**, the summit of the Quirinale Hill. When Rome was in its infancy, the Sabine tribes had their stronghold on the Quirinale – the highest of the Seven Hills of Rome – and their war god Quirinus is remembered in its name. The four fountains are rather unusual – there's an interesting emphasis on dense foliage in a couple of them, and they certainly form a contrast to the Dioscuri.

5 Turn right, past the British Council on your left and lots of cute, quirky shops – there is delicious, good value *gelato* to be had at Sunshine. When you meet **Via Nazionale**, turn left. This is a grand street, looking up to the **Piazza della Repubblica** and down to the wedding-cake confection of the **Monumento a Vittorio Emanuele II**. Take the first right, **Via Napoli**, looking out on the corner for **St Paul's Within the Walls**. Built in the 1870s, this American Anglican-Episcopal church has, among other treasures, some exquisite mosaics by English Pre-Raphaelite Edward Burne-Jones. The rest of the street is generally unprepossessing, but there are some interesting buildings and a useful subterranean supermarket on your right (supermarkets are few and far between in Rome, so if you need to stock up on fruit and veg to cut through all those carbs you'll be eating, this is your chance). Then take the first left, **Via del Viminale**, and you'll see the **Teatro dell'Opera** on your left. Behind the 1950s façade is a plush 19thC interior, and the programme of ballet, opera and music is impressive – plus of course there's little or no language barrier with these entertainments.

6 Turn left past the Teatro on **Via Torino**, crossing Via Nazionale and continuing ahead as the road opens into **Piazza di San Bernardo**. On your right is the circular **San Bernardo**, built in 1598 in one of the corner rotundas of the vast Baths of Diocletian. The fabulous geometric roof inside is a surprise after the sober exterior, and unusually large statues of saints tower above you in alcoves in the wall. Across from the entrance is a dark, half-hidden room with electric candles and halos glowing – approach slowly and, before the automatic lights are triggered, take in the eerie, magical atmosphere. Opposite is the elaborate **Santa Susanna**, even more ornate on the inside, with paintings covering every inch of the wall and some intriguing *trompe l'oeil* work.

7 Coming out of Santa Susanna, take the road to the left of the large red and white building, **Via Vittorio Emanuele Orlando**. Go past the Planetario on your left (once an octagonal hall from the Diocletian baths) and you are in Piazza della Repubblica, stamped all over with Diocletian's legacy. The curve of the buildings which flank the piazza traces the shape of the *exedra*, the curved wall of the stadium in the baths. The façade of **Santa Maria degli Angeli**, which emphasizes the impressive scale of the structure, uses original Roman masonry from the entrance to their Great Hall.

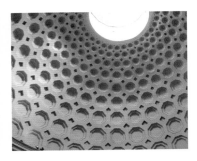

Geometric patterns on the ceiling of San Bernardo.

Pretty building along Via Torino.

Red and white building near Santa Susanna.

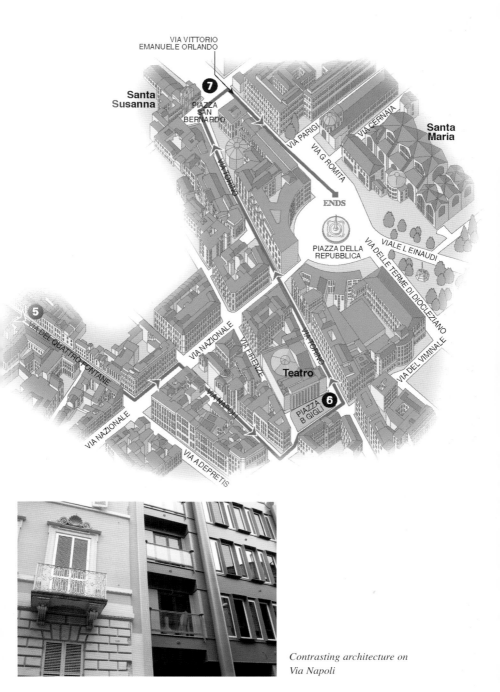

*Contrasting architecture on
Via Napoli*

8 Suppress any church fatigue you may be experiencing and go inside Santa Maria. The relatively modest exterior is misleading – this is a breathtakingly grand space, one to elevate the

John the Baptist sculpture in Santa Maria.

spirits. As a final revenge for Diocletian's Christian persecutions, Pope Pius IV had Michelangelo convert the great hall of the *tepidarium* into this church in the 1560s. The artist's respect for antiquity ensured that the glory of its vaulted interior was preserved, and it is one of the most striking examples of the pagan foundations of Christian Rome. Look up as you go in the modern bronze doors for the exquisite glass dome, installed in 2000 and aptly called 'Divinity in Light', by glass artist Narcissus Quagliata. The church interior is a fascinating mix of old and modern styles, paintings, sculptures and details. Particularly intriguing is the early 18thC bronze meridian line, flanked by panels showing signs of the zodiac. It was constructed by order of Pope Clement XI to determine the accuracy of the Gregorian reformation calendar, to predict the date of Easter – and to compete with the meridian line already laid down in San Petronio cathedral in Bologna. Roman baths tended to be built south facing, to make the most of the sun, so Santa Maria was in a perfect position for this complex sundial.

9 Outside, the piazza itself is a mixture of graceful sculpture and beeping horns. It was largely

Bronze doors of S. Maria.

redesigned at the turn of the century as an imposing introduction to the city for visitors arriving at Termini station. The **Fontana delle Naiadi** caused a stir when the nude figures – nymphs of the

Lampost in Piazza della Repubblica.

lakes, rivers, oceans and underground waters – were unveiled in the early 1900s. They do look a lot saucier than your average fountain statue and seem to be enjoying themselves hugely while the water god Glaucus wrestles with a fish in the centre. Superstitious Romans believe that driving a complete circle round the fountain brings good luck – with a car in Rome, you need it. Look at any row of parked cars and four out of five will be dented and scratched! If it's getting dark, linger a while in one of the cafés – the piazza lit up at night is a romantic sight. Otherwise, there's a metro stop in the piazza, or a left turn out of the church takes you to Termini, the main station.

Santa Maria interior.

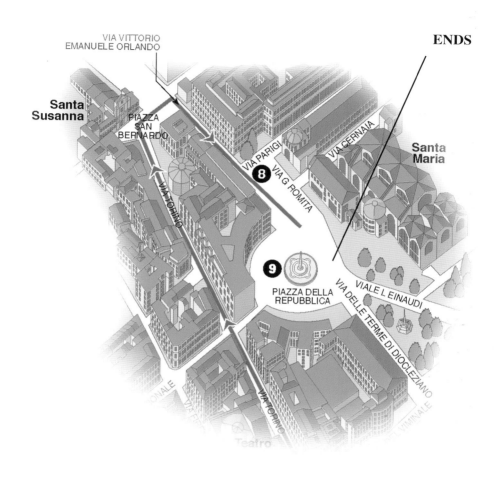

ENDS

VIA VITTORIO
EMANUELE ORLANDO

Santa
Susanna

PIAZZA
SAN
BERNARDO

VIA PARIGI

VIA G ROMITA

VIA CERNAIA

Santa
Maria

8

VIA TORINO

9

PIAZZA DELLA
REPUBBLICA

VIALE L EINAUDI

VIA DELLE TERME DI DIOCLEZIANO

VIA TORINO

VIA VIMINALE

Teatro

Santa Maria exterior.

Fontane Naiadi, Piazza Repubblica.

La Dolce Vita: From Via Veneto to the Trevi Fountain

It is perhaps difficult today to remember what an important filmmaking centre Rome was in the 1950 and 60s, when films such as *Roman Holiday, Three Coins in a Fountain, La Dolce Vita* and even parts of *Cleopatra* were made here, and stars like Cary Grant, Ava Gardner, Elizabeth Taylor and Frank Sinatra were regularly in the city, sometimes for long periods. Your walk begins where they spent most of their time, the Via Veneto, with its grand old hotels and pavement cafés. Now there is little left of such glamour, although the names of the hotels, bars and restaurants in the street remain the same and still draw numerous but visitors. You will then pass the usual selection of baroque palaces and churches, the principal collection of paintings in the city, beautiful statuary, an extremely macabre arrangement of human bones, a peaceful and concealed cloister, an obelisk

The Trevi Fountain.

and several famous fountains. The whole area is geared to the requirements of the tourist, with an unusually dense supply of *gelaterie*, bars, restaurants at all levels of elegance and expense, as well as plenty of shops, smart and otherwise: jewellers, tailors, shoes – almost everything in fact.

> ■ **ENDS**
> The Trevi Fountain.
> Nearest metro stop: Barberini.

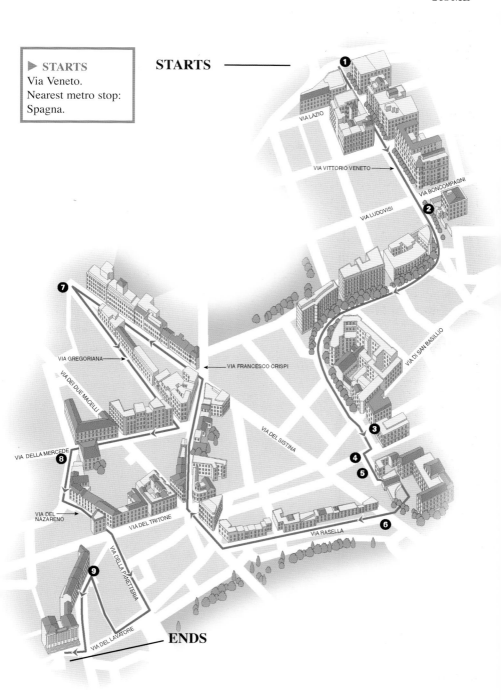

LA DOLCE VITA: FROM VIA VENETO TO THE TREVI FOUNTAIN

1 The **Via Veneto** is an elegant shady treelined boulevard, with wide pavements and street cafés, dating to the end of the 19th century/beginning of the 20th century. You start right outside **Harry's Bar**, an offshoot of the Venetian original, and given the length of today's route and the number of steep streets you will have to walk up and down, it might be a good idea to fortify yourself at the beginning. Down the street (no.114) is **Palombi**, once a bakery and now both bakery and restaurant, excellent for reasonable and light lunches. At no. 90 you come to the **Café de Paris**, one of the famous establishments of the Dolce Vita days, but a bit sad today. Across the road is the once equally famous **Caffè Doney** and the **Excelsior Hotel**, where kings and stars used to rub shoulders.

2 Passing the enormous American embassy on the left, the street curves down quite steeply to the right, and after some 300 m, on the left at **no. 27**, you will come to a flight of steps leading up to a church, **S. Maria della Concezione** (1626-30). On the right is the entrance to the **Capuchin crypt**, well worth visiting for the imaginative, ingenious and extremely macabre decoration using human bones. The walls and ceilings are adorned with whole skeletons, piles of skulls, chandeliers of rib

STARTS

VIA LAZIO

VIA VITTORIO VENETO →

VIA BONCOMPAGNI

VIA LUDOVISI

VIA DI SAN BASILLIO

FRANCESCO CRISPI

bones, tasteful patterns of vertebrae and hip bones, and other bewildering inventions. Children love it, but so do most adults. However, the serious visitor should also enter the church above as there are a number of very fine paintings inside, most notably in the first chapel on the right. Here you will find the swashbuckling *Saint Michael the Archangel tramples on Satan* (Guido Reni, 1635) and in the same chapel

Hotel Excelsior.

Fountain in Piazza Barberini.

Gerrit van Honthorst's *The Mocking of Christ* (c.1617), while in the first chapel on the left is *Ananias restores St Paul's Sight* (c.1631) by Pietro da Cortona.

❸ Further down the street on the same side is the charming **Fountain of the Bees** (1644), designed by Bernini. The fountain is indeed decorated with bees and you will come upon many more of them in this area, as they were the symbol of the Barberini family and their Pope, Urban VIII (1623-44), whose palace towers over the whole of

Fountain of the Tritons.

this square (**Piazza Barberini**). They were very energetic, extravagant builders and great patrons of Bernini, who rewarded them with some of his most fertile designs, such as the Baldacchino in St Peter's (also covered in bees, if you look closely).

❹ In the middle of the square stands another fountain designed by the great man, the **Fountain of the Triton** (1637). It is not easy to access on account of the swirling traffic and lack of pedestrian crossings. However, make the effort in order to examine up close the ingenious and elaborate base of dolphins, keys and bees, all twisting together and holding up the muscular figure of the triton, blowing into a conch shell trumpet.

Fountain of the Bees.

5 From here take the steep **Via delle Quattro Fontane** to the imposing railings and gates leading into the magnificent **Barberini palace**, dating to the 1620s and 30s and the work of three great architects, Carlo

Palazzo Barberini.

Maderno, Bernini and Borromini. Here the principal Italian state collection of paintings up to 1700 is - housed, but before entering, look at the fountain in front of the building and wander through the grand entrance, lined with antique statues, to the gardens and terraces at the back. Also look through the door on the right to see Borromini's exquisite elliptical spiral staircase in travertine which curls all the way up to the top of the building. The collection is extremely rich and some of the rooms exceedingly grand – a short list would include Raphael's highly alluring and seductive *Fornarina*, Holbein's terrifying, square *Henry VIII*, Caravaggio's *Judith Beheading Holofernes*, also terrifying, and *Christ and the Woman Taken in Adultery* by Tintoretto, with extraordinary perspective effects. Take in the enormous, mind-blowing great saloon, the height of two floors, whose ceiling is decorated with the *Triumph of Divine Providence* by Pietro da Cortona. There are also a number of fine papal busts.

6 Opposite the gates is the **Via Rasella**, sloping downwards. Turn right at the

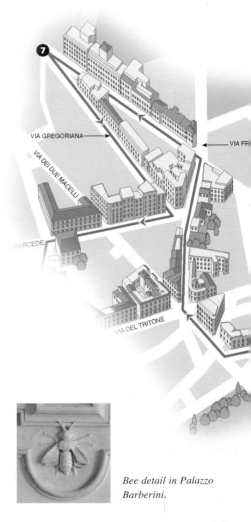

Bee detail in Palazzo Barberini.

bottom, cross the chaotic **Via del Tritone** and start climbing the **Via Francesco Crispi**. Halfway, pause to look down the **Via Capo le Case** to the left for a view of the striking belltower of **S. Andrea delle Fratte** which we will be coming to soon. Continue on up to the **Via Sistina**, where you turn left. This street is named after Pope

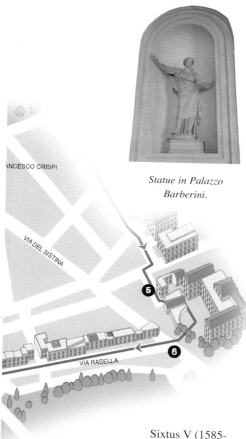

Statue in Palazzo Barberini.

Plaque on Bernini's house.

❼ Then take a sharp turn left down the extremely desirable **Via Gregoriana**, and at the bottom turn right towards the church we saw from a distance, S. Andrea delle Fratte. It was built during the first half of the 17th century, partly by Borromini, to whom is owed the fantastical belltower (look at the buffalo heads at the very top, a symbolic tribute to the patron, the noble Del Bufalo family). The inside is awash in coloured marbles, but the reasons for entering are two very fine and large statues by Bernini, of angels holding symbols of Christ's passion: on the left the crown of thorns, and on the right the scroll from the cross. On the other side of the church is a door leading into a cloister, a miraculously peaceful spot in a very busy part of the city. At the centre a moss and fern covered fountain quietly drips, surrounded by citrus and loquat trees. Leaving by the door on the right, look across the street at the large and sobre palace at **Via della Mercede no. 12 a**, which was the family residence of Bernini. He had 12 children, and was a very prosperous artist over many decades. His home reflects both.

Sixtus V (1585-90), and cuts a straight line, up and down hill, from the top of the Spanish Steps to the great church of **S. Maria Maggiore** in the distance, with obelisks standing theatrically at both ends. At the top of the Via Sistina, look over the Spanish Steps, even if they are already covered in the 'Romantics and Retail' walk (page 66). You may wish to refresh yourself at one of the bars up here, or indeed, if you are feeling rich, go for a drink or meal at the stately **Hotel Hassler Villa Medici** on the right – the grandest of the old-fashioned five-star hotels, occupying the best location. The views from the rooftop restaurant are breathtaking.

8 Now turn left, down the **Via di S. Andrea delle Fratte** into the **Largo del Nazareno**. Bear left past the ancient school at no. 25, the oldest in Rome, along the **Via del Nazareno**. Risk your life crossing the Via del Tritone again, and take the **Via della Panetteria** opposite. At no. 42 is a famous icecream emporium, **S. Crispino**, more sophisticated and more expensive than Pica in Walk 11, but perhaps not as good and certainly not as authentically Roman. At the end is the **Via del Lavatore**. Here turn right, past the picturesque and excellent food shop at **no. 31** (famous for its cheese selection), and then turn almost immediately right again down the **Vicolo Scavolino** to the end. This brings you to the **Piazza Accademia di S. Luca**, named after the academy for artists housed in the **Palazzo Carpegna** (no. 77). It has existed for centuries, and many of its members gave or bequeathed works to it. Enter the building, much of it restructured by Borromini, including the main staircase, which is in fact a fascinating spiral ramp entered by way of the highly original, great floral swag you can see from the street. Go up to the top floor, where there is an exhibition of some of the works the Accademia owns. These include paintings by Van Dyck, Rubens, Pannini, and Baciccia, and a bust by Canova (of Napoleon).

Andrea delle Fratte fountain in cloister.

9 On coming out, take the **Via della Stamperia**. In spite of the general hubbub, you will soon make out the sound of water, as round the corner is one of Rome's greatest attractions, the exuberant and enchanting **Trevi Fountain**. Built over some 30 years, between 1732 – 62, by the architects Nicola Salvi and Giuseppe Pannini, this has delighted visitors to Rome ever since. It is quite irresistible – a magnificent combination of shapely sculptures, majestic ocean scenes and a constant abundance of

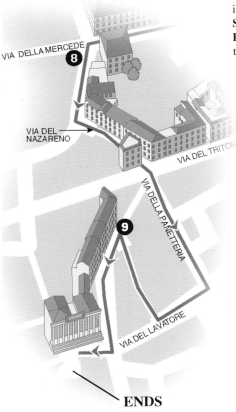

VIA DELLA MERCEDE

8

VIA DEL NAZARENO

VIA DEL TRITONE

VIA DELLA PANETTERIA

9

VIA DEL LAVATORE

ENDS

water gushing, set in a small square that seems quite out of proportion. See how the fountain grows out of the back of the building (the walls of travertine come down all cut straight and start becoming rock formations). It is excessively popular, quite understandably so, and like some other attractions, is ideally visited early in the morning. The bars and cafés round here are neither peaceful nor good value, and if you are flagging it is worth walking at least another five minutes in almost any direction before stopping.

Andrea delle Fratte belltower.

Bernini's Angel holding the Crown of Thorns.

Palazzo Carpegna.

The Trevi Fountain.

Romantics and Retail: Around the Spanish Steps

You certainly don't go to the Spanish Steps to engage with nature as John Keats and his Romantic contemporaries sought to do. It's one of the most popular tourist spots in Rome and, accordingly, a teeming mass of sightseers and street vendors. This is in part thanks to Keats himself, who died in the lovely pink-stuccoed building at the base of the steps – it is now something of a literary pilgrimage site. However, if you resign yourself in advance to the photo-snapping hordes, you won't be disappointed – it's still easy to imagine the poet, before tuberculosis confined him to his bed, lingering on the grand, sweeping steps. He said he could hear the constantly flowing water of the Barcaccia fountain from his bed (see point ❷) – perhaps it influenced his final epitaph for himself, inscribed on his gravestone: 'Here lies one whose name was writ in water'. You'll probably need sunglasses for this walk, which passes through a

number of glaringly white piazzas, with some cool and shady parks for contrast. Romans tended to build their piazzas for the 'wow' factor – whether it was as a memorial to themselves or as an imposing introduction to their city – and most are as impressive now as they would have been hundreds of years ago.

Once you've had your fill of architectural grandeur, turn your steps towards opulence of a different kind: the haughty, high-end shops which line Via del Corso, Via del Babuino and Piazza Spagna. All the big guns are there, and they make for extremely enjoyable window-shopping.

The Spanish Steps.

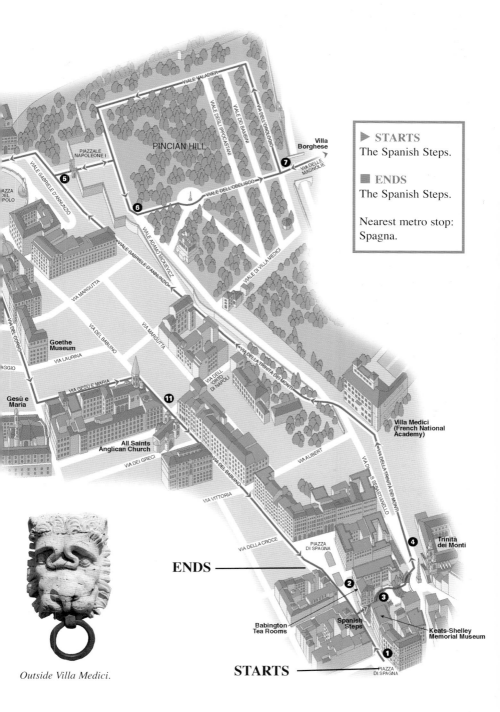

PINCIAN HILL

Villa
Borghese

PIAZZALE
NAPOLEONE I

VIALE VALADIER

VIALE DEGLI IPPOCASTANI

VIALE DEI BAMBINI

VIALE DELL'OROLOGIO

VIALE DELL'OBELISCO

VIA DELLE
MAGNOLIE

5

6

7

VIALE GABRIELE D'ANNUNZIO

PIAZZA
DEL
POLO

VIALE ADAMO MICKIEVICZ

VIALE GABRIELE D'ANNUNZIO

VIALE DI VILLA MEDICI

VIA MARGUTTA

VIA DEL BABUINO

VIA MARGUTTA

VIA DEL CORSO

Goethe
Museum

VIA LAURINA

VIALE DELLA TRINITA DEI MONTI

VIA DELL'
ORTO
DI NAPOLI

Gesù e
Maria

VIA GESÙ E MARIA

11

All Saints
Anglican Church

VIA DEI GRECI

VIA DEL BABUINO

VIA ALIBERT

VIA DELLA TRINITA DEI MONTI

Villa Medici
(French National
Academy)

VIA D. S. SEBASTIANELLO

VIA VITTORIA

VIA DELLA CROCE

PIAZZA
DI SPAGNA

4

Trinità
dei Monti

ENDS ——————

2

3

Babington
Tea Rooms

Spanish
Steps

Keats-Shelley
Memorial Museum

1

STARTS ——————

PIAZZA
DI SPAGNA

Outside Villa Medici.

▶ **STARTS**
The Spanish Steps.

■ **ENDS**
The Spanish Steps.

Nearest metro stop:
Spagna.

❶ From Spagna metro station, turn left into the **Piazza di Spagna** and almost immediately you will find yourself at the base of the **Spanish Steps** (properly called the Scalinata di Trinità), built in 1726 by Francesco De Sanctis to link the Spanish Embassy to the Trinità dei Monti church. On the right, at the base, is the house where John Keats lived for a few months before dying of consumption, as the disease was then called, in 1821, at the age of 25. The façade is unchanged, and it is now the **Keats-Shelley Memorial Museum**, a moving shrine to the English Romantics.

❷ To the left of the steps are the **Babington Tea Rooms**, established in 1893 by two English ladies, at a time when tea could only otherwise be purchased in pharmacies. It is a little corner of England in an otherwise decidedly un-English Piazza, and you could enjoy a well-earned cup of tea and cake here at the end of the walk. At the foot of the steps, the Barcaccia Fountain dribbles water from the prow and poop of a sinking ship. The popular legend behind the design is that the Piazza di Spagna once flooded so badly that a boat drifted into it, and was left marooned once the waters receded. It's a cute story, but one to take with a pinch of salt.

❸ Walk up the steps towards the towering white **Trinità dei**

English tea rooms.

Villa Medici (French National Academy)

VIA ALIBERT

VIA DI S SEBASTIANELLO

VIA DELLA TRINITÀ DEI MONTI

PIAZZA DI SPAGNA

❹

Trinità dei Monti

❷

Babington Tea Rooms

❸

Spanish Steps

Keats-Shelley Memorial Museum

❶

PIAZZA DI SPAGNA

STARTS

Monti, almost blinding on a sunny day. In front is one of Rome's 19 obelisks which, despite the Egyptian hieroglyphs, is in fact a 2ndC Roman pastiche moved here in 1789 from the Gardens of Sallust. The French king Louis XII ordered the building of twin-towered Trinità dei Monti, with its stuccoed façade by Carlo Maderno, in 1502. It is in a privileged position – check out the magnificent rooftop view from the balustraded terrace – and, inside, provides a refreshing contrast to the mania of the steps. In the second chapel is *The Deposition*, by Michelangelo's pupil Daniele da Volterra, which the 17thC French artist Pouisson thought to be the third greatest painting in the world.

❹ Coming out of the church, turn right on to the **Via della Trinità dei Monti**. You

Bust along Trinita dei Monti.

Keats-Shelley Memorial Museum.

Cairoli Brothers statue.

will go past the 16thC **Villa Medici** (look out for the nearby column which records Galileo's house arrest in the villa) on your right, now the French National Academy. English tours of the house and gardens take place at 11.45am as this guide went to press. Continue onwards, past the curious gun-wielding statue (a melodramatic 19thC monument to the Cairoli brothers, a pair of Garibaldian heroes who fell trying to enter Rome in 1867), and the road splits into two. Take the lower road, the **Viale Gabriele d'Annunzio**, and follow it almost to the end, where you will see a giant fountain above you on the right. Just past this and bearing slightly right is a statue of a lion at the edge of a grove or small park of trees on a slope. Head towards and follow one of the various paths upwards to the steps next to the apricot wall (there is a useful public toilet over on the left).

Around Trinita dei Monti.

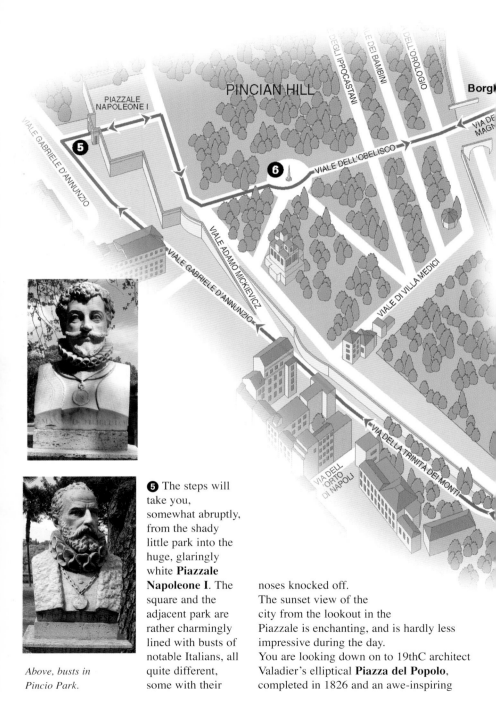

Above, busts in Pincio Park.

5 The steps will take you, somewhat abruptly, from the shady little park into the huge, glaringly white **Piazzale Napoleone I**. The square and the adjacent park are rather charmingly lined with busts of notable Italians, all quite different, some with their noses knocked off. The sunset view of the city from the lookout in the Piazzale is enchanting, and is hardly less impressive during the day.

You are looking down on to 19thC architect Valadier's elliptical **Piazza del Popolo**, completed in 1826 and an awe-inspiring introduction to the city for visitors entering from the north.

Villa hese

⑥ Turn back to the Piazzale Napoleon I and wander through it on to the **Viale dell'Obelisco,** heading towards the obelisk. Moved to the Pincio hill in 1822, it is a Roman copy, one of the many monuments that a grieving Emperor Hadrian erected to his drowned lover, Antinous. Stroll past the obelisk into the park, a pleasant place to eat your lunch and watch the inevitable street performers – there is often a team of rollerbladers showing off their astonishing

Seemingly twin churches in Piazza del Popolo.

Left, sign in Pincio Park.

Piazzale Napoleone I.

footwork. The Pincian hill has been a popular site for gardens since the Roman Epicurean Lucullus built his here in the 1st century A.D. The layout you see today is another of Valadier's designs, with its wide promenades shaded by tall planes, pines and evergreen oaks.

Piazza del Popolo

❼ To visit the **Villa Borghese** (not shown on map), with its beautiful English-style gardens and art gallery, go straight ahead at the end of the Via dell'Obelisco on to the **Via delle Magnolie** and follow the signs. Our route turns left on to the **Via dell'Orologio**, following it as it curves left and becomes the **Viale Valadier**. Look out for the delightful, grubby waterclock on your left, built in the 19th century by a Dominican monk, and the puppet theatre, which has regular shows. Continue ahead and back into the Piazza Napoleone I, from where you retrace your way down the steps meandering through the trees, past the lion statue, and bearing sharply to the right as far as the first curve in the road. At this point take the steep flight of steps leading down into the Piazza del Popolo. Unfortunately, at this scale, the map does not show exactly what you will see on the ground. There is a balustrade running along the edge of Piazzale Napoleone I, looking out over the Piazza del Popolo and towards St Peter's. The flight of steps leading to the park/grove is on the right side of the Piazzale Napoleone I, at the corner of the balustrade rather than in the middle of it.

Above, the lovely 19thC waterclock on Viale Valadier.

❽ The Piazza del Popolo is an energetic jumble of tourists, buskers and local kids set against a background of cool white grandeur, a fascinating place for people-watching and basking in the sunshine.

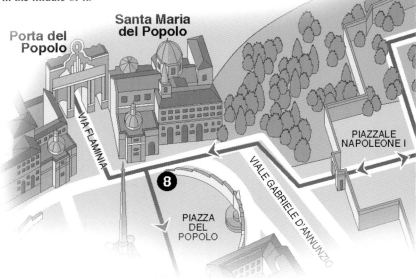

Porta del
Popolo

Santa Maria
del Popolo

VIA FLAMINIA

PIAZZALE
NAPOLEONE I

❽

PIAZZA
DEL
POPOLO

VIALE GABRIELE D'ANNUNZIO

Lion-head fountain.

Sphinx at the steps to the Piazza del Popolo.

The monumental gateway at the northern end is the 17thC **Porta del Popolo**, built to welcome Queen Cristina of Sweden, a Catholic convert, to Rome. Behind the gate, the ancient **Via Flaminia**, built in 220 BC, starts its long journey across Italy. Beside it huddles the early Renaissance façade of

Santa Maria del Popolo, built on an 11thC chapel erected to excorcise the malign spirit of Nero, whose ashes are reputedly buried hereabouts. The modest exterior hides a superb collection of art treasures, including Caravaggio's *Crucifixion of St Peter* and Raphael's sublime **Chigi chapel**.

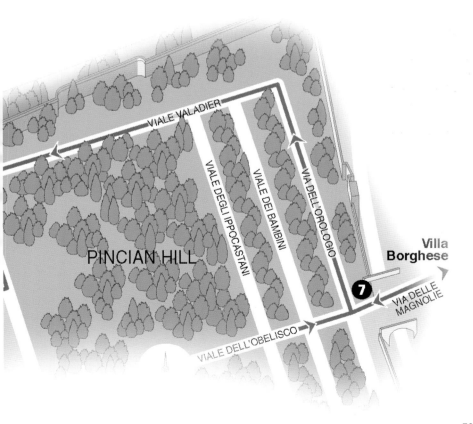

9 Moving towards the centre of the square you come face to face with the 3,000-year-old **obelisk**, which Augustus brought from Heliopolis to decorate the Circus Maximus. It was placed here a mere 400 years ago – you have to get used to a rather new scale of history in Rome. Head south away from the gate and obelisk towards the seemingly twin churches **Santa Maria dei Miracoli** and **Santa Maria in Montesanto**, and look carefully to see how architect Rainaldi's Baroque trickery makes two differently shaped buildings appear the same.

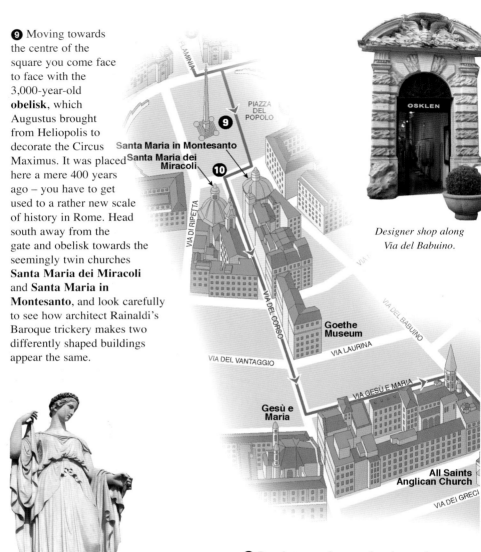

Designer shop along Via del Babuino.

Statue approaching Piazza del Popolo.

10 Pass between the two churches and set off down the **Via del Corso**, one of Rome's most popular shopping streets, with a good mix of high street and independent stores. It leads, straight as a die, to the Roman Forum (see 'Living Archaeology', pages 32-41). Look out for **no. 20** on your left, where Goethe stayed and fell in love with Rome, now a museum about his life and work. Just before Rainaldi's lavish High Baroque

Along Via del Corso.

Curious eroded fountain on Via del Babuino.

church of **Gesù e Maria** is the street of the same name – you want to turn left down here, but it's worth popping inside the church first, with its sumptuously painted arched roof. **Via Gesù e Maria**, a quiet, flower-lined street with some interesting shops, leads on to the **Via del Babuino**, another busy shopping street with some very expensive names.

Santa Maria in Montesanto.

11 Go past the neo-Gothic **All Saints** Anglican church on your right, a legacy of Rome's 19thC English ghetto, and keep going past designer shop after designer shop until you come back to the Spanish Steps and the metro on your left.

ENDS

In the Footsteps of Caravaggio:

Piazza del Popolo to

San Luigi dei Francesi

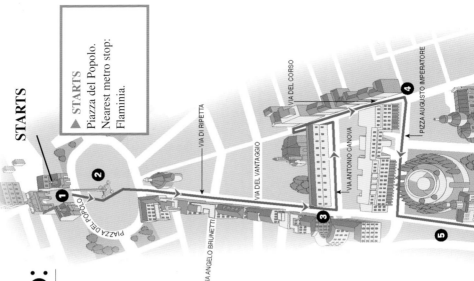

STARTS

▲ **STARTS**
Piazza del Popolo.
Nearest metro stop:
Flaminia.

PIAZZA DEL POPOLO

VIA DI RIPETTA

VIA DEL VANTAGGIO

VIA ANGELO BRUNETTI

VIA ANTONIO CANOVA

VIA DEL CORSO

PIAZZA AUGUSTO IMPERATORE

This walk is planned around some of the most sublime paintings ever created, and in its course ranges over Renaissance and Baroque churches, patrician palaces, ancient Roman monuments and striking 20thC architecture. You start from the Porta del Popolo, which leads into the distinctly theatrical Piazza del Popolo – from ancient times the entrance into the city for all travellers from the north. Today, this is linked by a straight road known as the Corso, right through the heart of the city. The piazza in its present form dates to the beginning of the 19th century and was the last piece of major urban redevelopment under papal rule. The three roads radiating from it are the Via del Babuino to the left, the Corso in the middle and the Via de Ripetta to the right. These were all built as part of major urban works carried out in the 16th century in an attempt to cut paths through some of the city's medieval disorder.

Y ou will be passing through some of the most desirable residential quarters of the modern city, mostly dating to the 15th and 16th centuries, and one of the very few parts of the centre to have been redeveloped in the 20th and 21st centuries, Piazza Augusto Imperatore.

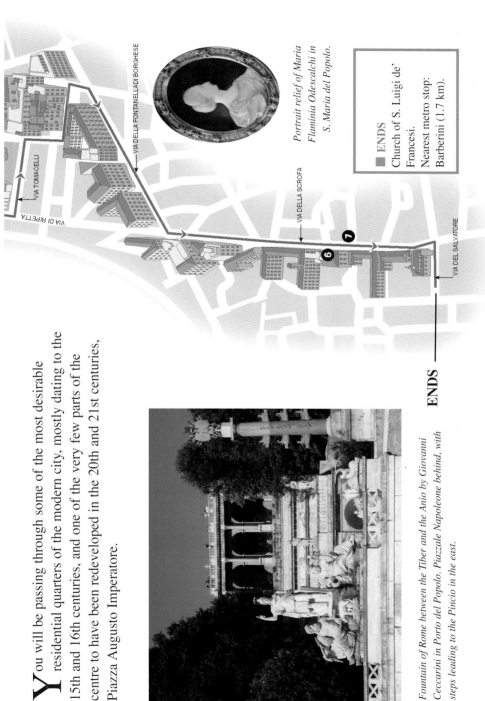

Portrait relief of Maria Flaminia Odescalchi in S. Maria del Popolo.

VIA DELLA FONTANELLA DI BORGHESE

VIA TOMACELLI

VIA DI RIPETTA

VIA DELLA SCROFA

VIA DEL SALVATORE

ENDS
Church of S. Luigi de' Francesi.
Nearest metro stop: Barberini (1.7 km).

ENDS

Fountain of Rome between the Tiber and the Anio by Giovanni Ceccarini in Porto del Popolo. Piazzale Napoleone behind, with steps leading to the Pincio in the east.

❶ With your back to the gate, climb the steps and enter the church on the left, **S. Maria del Popolo**, largely dating to the late 15th century and a veritable museum and gallery. Crowds head straight down to the Cesi chapel at the bottom left, in which two of Caravaggio's most celebrated paintings are displayed: *The Crucifixion of St Peter* and *The Conversion of St Paul*. They are indeed spectacular but there are plenty of other delights too. On the same side of the church, towards the entrance, is the private chapel of the Chigi family begun in 1513 to a design by Raphael, completed by Bernini in 1652-56. Two of the great sculptor's classic pieces are housed here: *Habakkuk and the Angel* and *Daniel in the Lion's Den*. Against the wall to the left of the chapel stands a poignant but delightfully rococo funerary monument to the young Maria Flaminia Odescalchi. Her portrait relief shows long-nosed features and an elaborate coiffure, highly redolent of ancient and aristocratic lineage; she died in 1771 at the age of 20, giving birth to her third child. In the rest of the church seek out frescoes by Pinturicchio and the only medieval stained glass in Rome (both in the chapel behind the altar screen), handsome Renaissance tombs and funerary monuments to assorted clerics, and the 16 Sicilian jasper columns in the resplendent Cybo chapel (second on the right of the church).

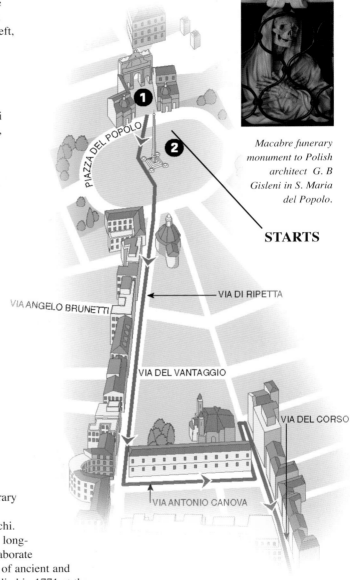

Macabre funerary monument to Polish architect G. B Gisleni in S. Maria del Popolo.

STARTS

❷ Back in the square, head towards the obelisk in the middle, dating to about 1200 BC and brought by Augustus from Hierapolis in Egypt to adorn the Circus Maximus. The four lion fountains at its base are Egyptian-style 19thC creations. Over on the far side of the square, give a quick glance at the attractive and apparently twin churches, (in fact, the dome on the left has 12 sides, whereas the dome on the right has 8, and neither church has much to see on the inside). Set off down the street on the right, **Via de Ripetta**. This is lined with a mix of rather superior and quirky little shops and all sorts of eating places. Worthy of mention are: **Buccone** at (no. 19/20), a wine shop and bar; the ironmongers **Toresi** (no. 26/27), with a remarkable range of wood chisels on display; the unnamed and conspicuously antiquated dollepair shop (**no. 29**); and the artist's materials emporium at no. 60, **Non Solo Arte**.

Above, Porta del Popolo.
Left, Decorative doors to S. Maria del Popolo.
Below, Fountain in Piazza del Popolo.

Obelisk in Piazza del Popolo.

79

❸ After some 300 m, you will come to the striking, horseshoe-shaped **Institute of Fine Arts** on the right. Here turn left along the **Via A. Canova**, named after the famous Venetian sculptor who had his studio at no. 16/17. The street is decorated with classical odds and ends and finishes at the **Via del Corso**. Slightly to the left, on the far side of the Corso, have a quick look into the church of **Gesù e Maria**. This is a richly decorated Baroque church, with walls covered in coloured marbles, lightened by animated sculptures of various members of the Bolognetti family, patrons of the church, who gesticulate and chat from little balconies over the elaborate confessionals.

The striking architecture of Ara Pacis.

American architect, Richard Meier, to house **Augustus's Altar of Peace**. This is an important historical record, exquisitely worked in white marble, and shows cortèges of members of Augustus's family and some unidentified figures. If you want to work them out, there are helpful illustrations. Walk down **Via Tomacelli**, then turn down the narrow **Via Monte d'Oro** and then left across the front of the enormous **Palazzo Borghese**, still in private hands and sadly not open to the public. Continue straight on along the **Via del Clementino** as far as the **Via della Scrofa**, where turn left. If hungry by this time, there are plenty of bars around, or in the nearby **Vicolo della Campana** you'll find what claims to be Rome's oldest restaurant, **La Campana**, at no. 18.

Interesting sculptural decorations on Via A. Canova.

❹ On down the Corso, take the **Via dei Pontefici** to the right, which leads into Fascist **Piazza Augusto Imperatore**, built 1937-40. All that remains of the once magnificent Mausoleum of Augustus lies in a somewhat depressing heap of brick in the middle. The emperor, who ruled 28 BC-14 AD, was buried here alongside close members of his family and descendants.

❺ However, your eye will be drawn to the large white building on the far side (building not shown on map), the conspicuous, if controversial museum designed by the

Palazzo Borghese.

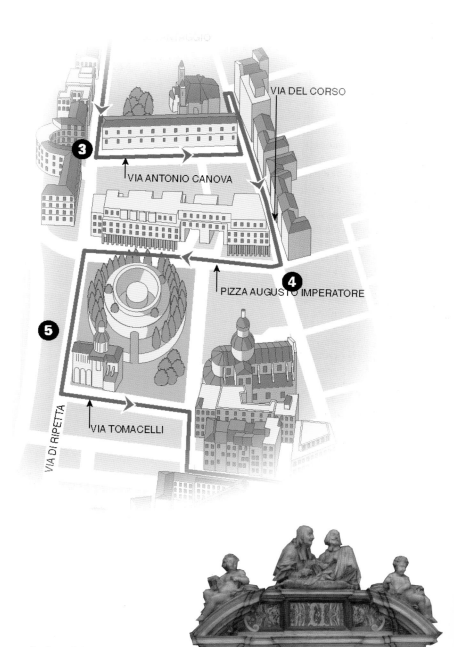

VIA DEL CORSO

VIA ANTONIO CANOVA

❸

PIZZA AUGUSTO IMPERATORE

❹

❺

VIA DI RIPETTA

VIA TOMACELLI

Sculptural detail in Gesù e Maria.

6 Further down the Via della Scrofa, to the right, you will soon come to the **Via, Piazza and church of S. Agostino**, fronted by an imposing flight of steps and severe façade, dating to the 15th century. Inside, on the left, is one of Caravaggio's most captivating works, *The Madonna of the Pilgrims* (1604-1606). The Madonna, whose features are those of the notorious and beautiful courtesan, Lena Antognetti, much admired by the powerful of the time, stands rather nonchalantly at the door of her house, clad in sumptuous velvet, holding a large baby, with two very grubby pilgrims kneeling in adoration before her. All is bathed in beautiful light. In the main aisle, third column on the left, is Raphael's fresco *The Prophet Isaiah*. According to folklore, the patron who commissioned the work from Raphael complained to Michelangelo about the cost. Raphael was very successful by this point, and was correspondingly expensive. However, Michelangelo came to view the work and crushingly decreed that the knee alone was worth the price. To the side of the main door is a statue known as the *Madonna of Childbirth*, a matronly figure reminiscent of classical goddesses, holding an extremely sturdy baby Jesus in a silver nappy. She remains a symbol of fertility – women come to pray in order to conceive and to ensure a

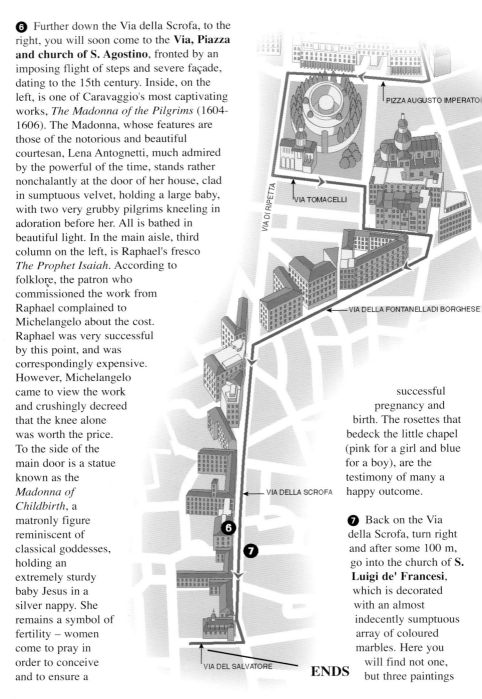

successful pregnancy and birth. The rosettes that bedeck the little chapel (pink for a girl and blue for a boy), are the testimony of many a happy outcome.

7 Back on the Via della Scrofa, turn right and after some 100 m, go into the church of **S. Luigi de' Francesi**, which is decorated with an almost indecently sumptuous array of coloured marbles. Here you will find not one, but three paintings

S. Agostino facade.

chariots and was later adopted as a symbol in Christian iconography. Martyrdom for the 'true' faith was seen as a victory. The figure slightly to the right of St Matthew, seen from behind and observing the scene, is supposedly the painter himself. After such a surfeit of genius, it might be wise to repair to one of the numerous bars in front of the **Pantheon**. Or, to sample some of the finest coffee in town, pop in to the **Tazza d'Oro**, just on the far side of the Pantheon square, or the **Caffè S. Eustachio**, in Piazza S. Eustachio, some 200 m ahead.

by Caravaggio, all based on the life of St Matthew and displayed in the last side chapel to the left of the church. On the left side of the chapel is *The Calling of St Matthew*, in which Jesus stands with St Peter, pointing towards the figure of St Matthew on the left of the picture. An extraordinary shaft of light cuts across the picture from right to left, illuminating St Matthew, a tax gatherer shown sitting at a table with his undesirable and brightly dressed associates. He is pointing to himself, about to rise and follow Jesus. On the back wall is *St Matthew in Old Age*, writing his gospel and conversing with an angel, who is enumerating with his fingers various incidents for Matthew to record in his gospel. For some reason, the stool on which he rests his knee is portrayed rocking on the edge of what looks like a stage. On the right of the chapel is the imagined scene *The Martyrdom of St Matthew* (there are no accounts of how he died), in which a violent and scantily clothed young man is about to deliver the *coup de grace* to the prostrate saint. An angel leans down from heaven proffering a palm branch – this was given in Roman times to the winner of

Madonna of Childbirth in S. Agostino.

83

Lost in the Folds of History: From the Pantheon to Palazzo Altemps

Today you range through a compact area crammed with some of the city's most famous monuments and sights. These include the best preserved of all ancient Roman buildings, one of the city's greatest medieval churches, some of Raphael's frescoes, several of the most celebrated Baroque creations by Borromini and Bernini, plus a sprinkling of squares and fountains. Throughout the walk look upwards from time to time in order to appreciate the architectural quality of the area, as there is a high concentration of beautiful yet modest buildings, with fine doors, window frames, cornices or courtyards. Do not expect to come across the picturesquely rundown, as this is one of the most desirable residential parts of the city, nor will you ever be off the beaten track – the Pantheon and the Piazza Navona are understandably crowded, and almost every street is lined with bars, restaurants and gelaterie. However, in the back streets leading off the Piazza Navona and the Via dei Coronari you will sense the Middle Ages and Renaissance, as you make your way along narrow passages and alleys and across small squares.

VIA TOR DI NONA

VIA DELL'ARCO DI PARMA

Casa di Fiammetta

ARCO DEGLI ACQUASPARTA

VIA ZANARDELLI

S. Salvatore

VICOLO DEI MARCHIGIANI

PIAZZA DI FIAMMETTA

VIA DELLA MASCHERO D'ORO

9

PIAZZA S. SALVATORE IN LAURO

VIA DEI CORON

Palazzo Lancellotti

LARG FEBC

S. Maria della Pace

8

VICOLO DELLA PACE

VIA DELLA PACE

VIA TOR MILLINA

7

VIA DI S. AGNESE

S. Agnese

St Sebastian

Palazzo Pamphilj

Palaz Brasc

■ **ENDS**
Piazza S. Apollinare.
Nearest metro stop: S. Pietro (2.7 km away).

ENDS

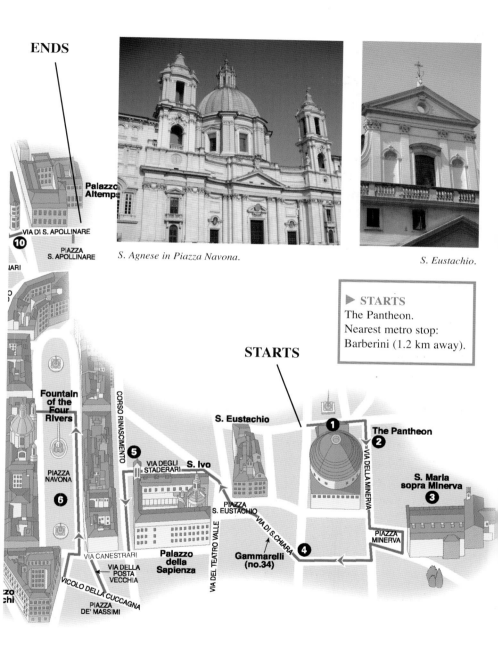

S. Agnese in Piazza Navona.

S. Eustachio.

▶ **STARTS**
The Pantheon.
Nearest metro stop:
Barberini (1.2 km away).

STARTS

VIA DI S. APOLLINARE

⑩

PIAZZA
S. APOLLINARE

**Palazzo
Altemps**

**Fountain
of the
Four
Rivers**

CORSO RINASCIMENTO

PIAZZA
NAVONA

⑥

⑤

VIA DEGLI
STADERARI

S. Ivo

S. Eustachio

PIAZZA
S. EUSTACHIO

①

The Pantheon
②

VIA DELLA MINERVA

**S. Maria
sopra Minerva**
③

PIAZZA
MINERVA

VIA CANESTRARI

VIA DELLA
POSTA
VECCHIA

VICOLO DELLA CUCCAGNA

PIAZZA
DE' MASSIMI

**Palazzo
della
Sapienza**

VIA DEL TEATRO VALLE

VIA DI S. CHIARA

**Gammarelli
(no.34)**

④

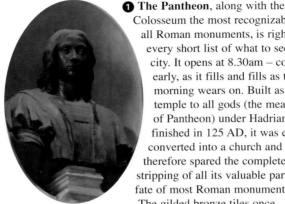

Bust of Raphael at the Pantheon.

❶ The Pantheon, along with the Colosseum the most recognizable of all Roman monuments, is rightly on every short list of what to see in the city. It opens at 8.30am – come early, as it fills and fills as the morning wears on. Built as a temple to all gods (the meaning of Pantheon) under Hadrian, finished in 125 AD, it was early converted into a church and therefore spared the complete stripping of all its valuable parts, the fate of most Roman monuments. The gilded bronze tiles once covering the dome were carried off to Constantinople and the bronze decorating the portico was removed by the Barberini pope, Urban VIII (1623-44), for making the Baldacchino in St Peter's and the odd cannon. Despite this, the Pantheon is the only great Roman monument in the city to survive in anything like its original form. Get right up close to the columns in the portico in order to appreciate their immensity, examine the bronze doors (much repaired but substantially the original ones), and gaze in awe at the great dome, the widest unsupported span until well on in the 20th century. Over to the left is the tomb of Raphael.

❷ Taking the **Via della Minerva** up the side of the building, you will soon come to the dignified **Piazza Minerva**, with the enchanting marble elephant at its centre holding up a small obelisk, a design by Bernini.

❸ The church here, **S. Maria sopra Minerva**, is satisfying architecturally (the only Gothic church in Rome) and also for its treasures. First amongst these is the Carafa chapel, bottom right, frescoed by Filippino Lippi (1488-93). On the back wall is an exquisite Annunciation scene, in which Mary learns she is expecting the son of God at the same time as Cardinal Oliviero Carafa, displaying an astonishing lack of humility, is presented to her. Above, the Virgin floats heavenwards, pushed up by a bevy of angels playing musical instruments. On the left glowers the family pope, Paul IV, scourge of Rome's Jewish community and much hated by the Roman populace. Behind the main altar are two magnificent papal tombs, to the Medici popes Leo X (1513-21) on the left and Clement VII (1523-34) on the right. On the left of the altar is a marble statue known as *Christ Arisen*, supposedly started by Michelangelo but not finished by him. The upper body displays some of the physical perfection associated with the great master, but the hips and lower quarters are distinctly clumsy. Back outside, look at the plaques on the façade showing the levels reached by some of the city's great floods. They are impressive, and while the one clearly marked December 1870 seems realistic, the highest one, several feet above, may well be an exaggeration.

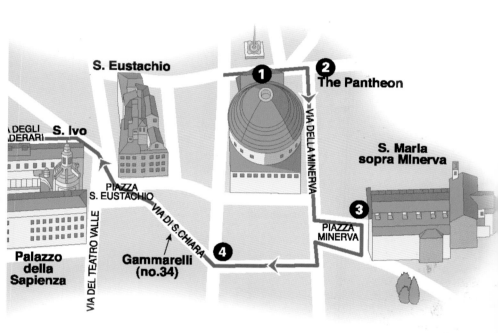

S. Eustachio

1

2
The Pantheon

DEGLI
DERARI   **S. Ivo**

**S. Marla
sopra Minerva**

VIA DELLA MINERVA

PIAZZA
S. EUSTACHIO

VIA DI S. CHIARA

**S. Marla
sopra Minerva**

3

PIAZZA
MINERVA

VIA DEL TEATRO VALLE

**Palazzo
della
Sapienza**

**Gammarelli
(no.34)**

4

4 Taking the **Via di S. Chiara** on the far side, pause to look into the
window of the pope's official tailor, **Gammarelli** (no. 34), where you will
see on sale some unique items of clothing. Continue to the end. This will
bring you into the **Piazza S. Eustachio**, named after the sweet little
church on the right, topped by a stag's head (St Eustace, out hunting
with his friend Hadrian, was converted by a vision of the cross
appearing between the antlers of a stag he was about to down – his
eventual fate was to be roasted alive in a bronze bull). Pass the **Caffè
S. Eustachio** on the left, very famous for its coffee. Here either bear
slightly right and then up the **Via degli Staderari**, passing the
enormous Roman granite basin, serving as a fountain, or turn left
along the **Via del Teatro Valle**, and almost immediately through the
doors of **number VI/VII**, into an elegant courtyard, porticoed on
two levels. This is the **Palazzo della Sapienza** (wisdom),
originally the Vatican university, founded in 1303, but much of its
present form dates to the 16th and 17th centuries. Its most famous
feature is the church at one end, **S. Ivo** (1642-52), designed by
Borromini, with a fantastical spiral lantern.

*Bernini's elephant
sculpture in Piazza
Minerva.*

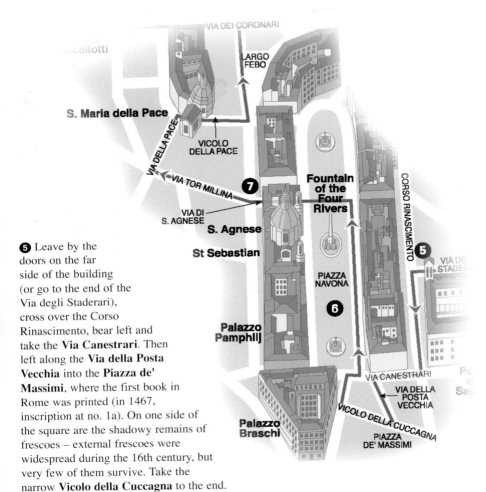

5 Leave by the doors on the far side of the building (or go to the end of the Via degli Staderari), cross over the Corso Rinascimento, bear left and take the **Via Canestrari**. Then left along the **Via della Posta Vecchia** into the **Piazza de' Massimi**, where the first book in Rome was printed (in 1467, inscription at no. 1a). On one side of the square are the shadowy remains of frescoes – external frescoes were widespread during the 16th century, but very few of them survive. Take the narrow **Vicolo della Cuccagna** to the end.

In front rises the huge **Palazzo Braschi**, the last palace on such a scale erected by a pope as a family residence – in this case Pius VI (1775-99). The palace has a particularly fine main staircase and now serves as the **Museo di Roma** (entrance on the far side), containing an interesting selection of portraits, busts, outfits and so on, illustrating Roman life during the 17th-19th centuries, with an emphasis on aristocratic, church circles, including some portraits of magnificently jowly members of the clergy.

6 To the right is the **Piazza Navona**, the most beautiful and theatrical large square in Rome, long and narrow, the buildings all round standing on the remains of Domitian's stadium (81-86 AD). To the left is the enormous **Palazzo Pamphilj**, family home of Innocent X (1644 -55), which includes the spectacular and sumptuously decorated church of **S. Agnese** and the block beyond it. Agnese was supposedly martyred in this square – inside the church, on the right, is the dramatic statue of the saint being consumed by flames, and for good measure, on the right, a somewhat camp St Sebastian, transfixed with arrows. There is also a small chapel dedicted to the skull of S. Agnese. This block is largely (but not wholly) the work of Borromini, but the extraordinary **Fountain of the Four Rivers**, rising in front of the church with its obelisk, was conceived by Bernini. The 'four rivers' were the longest of the continents that were recognized at the time. America's River Plate (Bernini got it wrong) is identified by a strange, half armadillo, half alligator, to one side and a cactus to the other. Europe's Danube is represented by a horse, while Asia's Ganges, is symbolized by a somewhat corroded snake. Finally, a lion and palm tree signify the Nile in Africa. Almost the whole square is surrounded by clamorous bars and restaurants, and the centre is filled with 'artists' of one description and another – this is also somewhere it is worth getting up early for.

❼ Taking the **Via di S. Agnese** just on the other side of the fountain, and continuing up the **Via Tor Millina**, you will soon come to a little square. On the corner is the fashionable **Bar della Pace**, swathed in greenery, much loved by film stars, and to right the **Via della Pace**. At the end is the delightful church of **S. Maria della Pace**, fronted by an exquisite semicircular portico. The main body of the church dates to the 1480s, the portico being added in 1656. The hours of opening are strange (and frequently change), but it is worth making the effort to get in just to see Raphael's famous Sibyls over the top of the chapel of one of his main patrons, Agostino Chigi.

Above left, River Nile. Above right, River Ganges. Far right, River Plate. Right, River Danube.

8 To the right of the church is a little alley, **Vicolo della Pace**, which curves round to the right. At the end turn left into and through the **Largo Febo**, and then left up the **Via dei Coronari**, an elegant, straight street, full of fine buildings and many antique shops. Past a small square with fountain, the **Via Lancellotti** and the sobre **Palazzo Lancellotti**, you come to the drab **Piazza S. Salvatore** in Lauro on the right and the slightly pompous church of **S. Salvatore**, whose inside does not really merit investigation. But to the left of it is a door leading into the cloisters which are on an altogether different plane. The porter is watchful but usually lets you wander through the plain, peaceful cloisters and adjoining courtyard with dripping fountain at its centre, all dating to the end of the 15th century. If you ask the porter kindly, you may be allowed into the refectory to see the magnificent monument by Isaia da Pisa to the Venetian pope, Eugenio IV (1431-47). A discreet tip may help.

9 Take the **Vicolo dei Marchigiani** in the corner, then the **Via Tor di Nona** for a couple of blocks, right along the **Via dell'Arco di Parma**, and left down the **Via della Maschero d'Oro**, past another palace with faded outside fresco work (**no. 7**) and one with incised work (**no. 9**), as far as the passage on the left, the **Arco degli Acquasparta**. This leads to the much-restored but attractive 15thC **Casa di Fiammetta**, named after a famous courtesan of the time, which now houses the offices of some finance company. Pass round the house into the **Piazza di Fiammetta**, turn left and head towards the large palace rearing up ahead.

The corner of Palazzo Altemps.   *S. Salvatore in Lauro.*

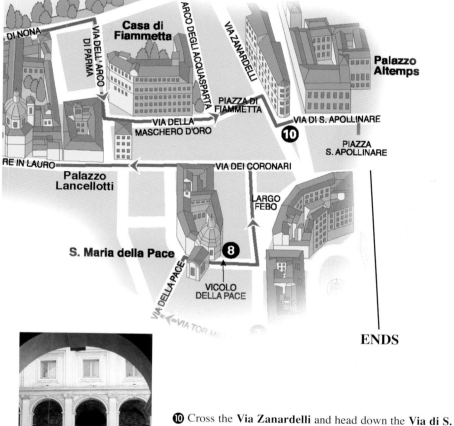

⑩ Cross the **Via Zanardelli** and head down the **Via di S. Apollinare**, past the imposing **Palazzo Altemps** (late 15thC), and its very beautiful porticoed courtyard, now an archaeological museum. It contains many of the most famous antique sculptures of the city, the greatest perhaps being the Ludovisi Throne. Entrance is in the **Piazza S. Apollinare**.

Palazzo Altemps courtyard.

Life at the Top: Noble Palazzi from Piazza Venezia to Piazza San Lorenzo in Lucina

Over the course of this walk you will pass some of the largest and most sumptuous private palaces in Europe, still occupied by the families that built them. The current residents all have a pope amongst their forebears – papal nepotism was rife between 1450 and 1800, and popes generally provided well for their immediate relatives. You will also see a fairly plain palace, in which the last of the royal House of Stuart lived; the family rather sadly resided in Rome where they finally lost hope of returning to the British throne. The walk also takes in: the political heart of the city, Parliament; the official residence of the Prime Minister; beautiful squares; a varied array of churches with works of art, relics and other curiosities; a couple of important and imposing Roman monuments, and an Egyptian obelisk. The whole area is upmarket,with plenty of fancy shops and numerous high-class bars and restaurants. Two of the best can be found in the traffic-free square in at the end of the walk – an excellent place to have a drink and light meal after quite an arduous route.

S. Lorenzo in Lucina facade.

Statue near S. Marco.

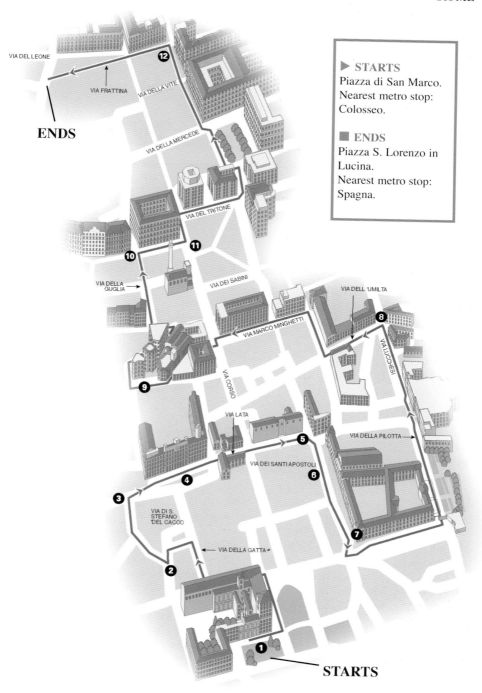

VIA DEL LEONE

VIA FRATTINA

VIA DELLA VITE

ENDS

VIA DELLA MERCEDE

VIA DEL TRITONE

► **STARTS**
Piazza di San Marco.
Nearest metro stop:
Colosseo.

■ **ENDS**
Piazza S. Lorenzo in
Lucina.
Nearest metro stop:
Spagna.

VIA DELLA
GUGLIA

VIA DEI SABINI

VIA DELL 'UMILTA

VIA MARCO MINGHETTI

VIA LUCCHESI

VIA CORSO

VIA LATA

VIA DELLA PILOTTA

VIA DEI SANTI APOSTOLI

VIA DI S.
STEFANO
DEL CACCO

VIA DELLA GATTA

STARTS

93

❶ We start in a corner of Rome soaked in Venetian associations – the **Piazza S. Marco**, dominated by the church of **S. Marco** (mainly 1460s, with a magnificent ceiling, and 9thC mosaics). This is built into one side of the enormous **Palazzo Venezia**, begun by the Venetian Pope Paul II (1464-71), and once serving as the residence of Venetian representatives in Rome. It subsequently underwent many vicissitudes, at one time housing Mussolini's offices, and has ended up as one of the most idiosyncratic and interesting museums in the city (featuring pictures, porcelain, armour, exquisite bronzes, stone). Following the side on Piazza Venezia, pass under the balcony from which Mussolini used to address the crowds, turn left along the **Via del Plebiscito**, and once past the entrance to the museum, right down the **Via della Gatta** and into the **Piazza Grazioli**, glancing up at the little stone cat (which gives the street its name) on the corner. On the left is the **Palazzo Grazioli**. This rather nondescript building may not be of much architectural interest, but it has achieved a certain notoriety as the private residence of the current Italian Prime Minister, Silvio Berlusconi.

❷ Take the **Via S. Stefano del Cacco** leading off to the right of the **Palazzo Grazioli**, and follow it for 100 m as far as the big marble foot (the **Piè di Marmo**), a remnant of a colossal female statue.

❸ Turn right along the **Via del Piè di Marmo** (on the other side of the road, no. 21/22, is a famous and very old-fashioned handmade chocolate shop, **Moriondo e Gariglio**), and into the broad **Piazza del Collegio Romano**, named after the enormous Jesuit seminary whose bulk occupies the whole of the left side. The building dates from the last decades of the 16th century, and from here the missionaries and teachers trained according to the

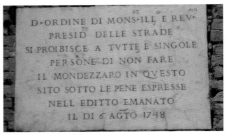

Top, the water carrier fountain on Via Lata. Below, a plaque near the fountain forbidding visitors from dropping litter.

precepts of the founder of the order, St Ignatius, who set out to convert and educate the whole world.

❹ On the opposite side of the square is the equally vast bulk of the **Palazzo Doria Pamphilj**, owned by the family which produced Pope Innocent X (1644-55), whose grasping sister-in-law, Donna Olimpia, was chiefly responsible for setting the family up in such style. Inside the palace is one of the most extraordinary private collections of paintings in the world, including Caravaggio's *Rest on the Flight into Egypt* and *Penitent Magdalen*, Titian's *Head of John the Baptist*, a double portrait by Raphael, *The Deposition* by Hans Memling and, most famous of all, the *Portrait of Innocent X* by Velasquez. These are all world-class paintings, but there are hundreds more and several spectacular busts, including one of the dreadful Donna Olimpia by Algardi, all displayed in a sumptuously decorated gallery. Entrance is round the corner at **Via del Corso**, no. 305. Leave the square by the short **Via Lata** over on the far side. On the left there is a decrepit statue of an old man holding a water barrel (the water is delicious) and on the right is the church of **S. Maria in Via Lata**, richly decorated, and architecturally distinguished, designed by Pietro da Cortona. Cross the Corso and take the **Via dei Ss. Apostoli** on the far side and at the end turn slightly right.

Above, San Marco facade.

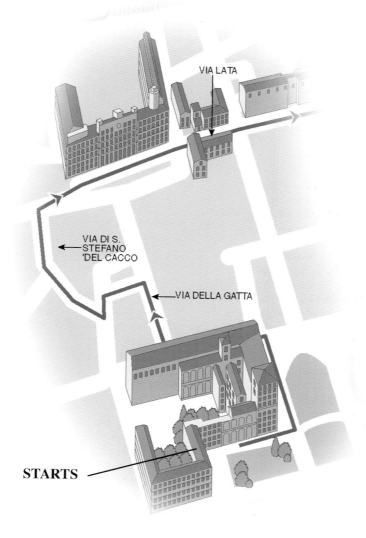

VIA LATA

VIA DI S. STEFANO 'DEL CACCO

VIA DELLA GATTA

STARTS

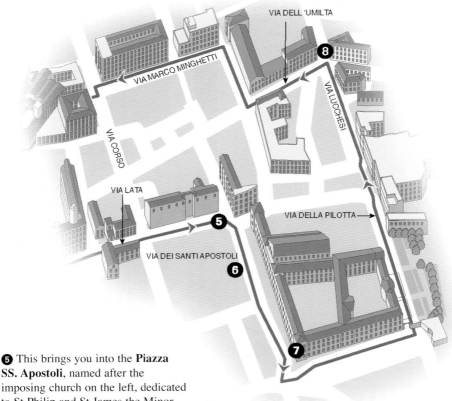

⑤ This brings you into the **Piazza SS. Apostoli**, named after the imposing church on the left, dedicated to St Philip and St James the Minor, whose remains rest in an antique sarcophagus under the main altar. At one end of the portico of the church is the funerary plaque by Antonio Canova to Giovanni Volpato, in which a seated female figure, Amicitia (friendship), weeps before the portrait of the dead man. This work dates from 1807 and is exquisite in both conception and execution. At number no. 49 is the **Palazzo Balestra**, in which the Stuart family lived after James II was forced to abdicate. Here his son, who styled himself as James III, took up residence and it remained the seat of the Stuart court-in-exile for over two generations: James III's sons, Charles Edward, Bonnie Prince Charlie, and his brother, Henry Stuart, were born and died in the palazzo.

⑥ Across the square from the church at nos 80 and 81 is the stately **Palazzo Odescalchi,** not visitable, occupied by the heirs of Pope Innocent XI (1676-89).

Galleria Sciarra.

Funerary plaque of Amiticia (friendship) near SS. Apostoli.

❼ At the end, on the left, **nos. 53-68**, is the residence of the Colonna family (Pope Martin V, 1417-31), generally thought to be the grandest in Rome. They have lived on this site for more than 700 years, although much of the palace dates to the 17th and 18th century. There is an impressive collection of paintings here too, and although the works do not compare to the greatest Doria Pamphilj pictures, the rooms and halls in which they are displayed (particularly the Great Saloon), are astonishingly magnificent. To visit the gallery (open Saturdays only, 9 am-1 pm), turn left at the end of the **Piazza Ss. Apostoli**, up the **Via IV Novembre**, and take the first turning to the left along the **Via della Pilotta** to the entrance at no. 17. Continue along this delightful street, under the elegant stone bridges linking the palace to its spacious private gardens, stretching up the hill in a series of terraces. Then on through the **Piazza della Pilotta**, with the Vatican's Gregorian University on the right,

and along the **Via dei Lucchesi** on the far side, to the end and then left as far as the **Piazza dell'Oratorio** (about 100 m).

❽ Here turn right into the quaint **Galleria Sciarra**, a shopping precinct dating to the 1880s, attached to the back of the **Palazzo Sciarra** (now a bank). On the far right corner there survives a remarkably old-fashioned gentleman's outfitters and hatters, Viganò. Once through the Galleria Sciarra, turn left down the **Via Marco Minghetti**, past the tourist office, and back across the Via del Corso, down **Via Montecatini**. At the end turn right and into the most beautiful small square in the city, the **Piazza di S. Ignazio**, which looks almost like a theatre set. The square is overwhelmed by the enormous façade of the Jesuit church of S. Ignazio. This is a riot of marble and *lapis lazuli*, with magnificent *trompe l'oeil* frescoes by Andrea Pozzo, including the extraordinary dome, which looks completely realistic until you stand directly underneath – it then falls flat.

Piazza di S.Ignazio

97

Temple of Hadrian.

❾Taking the **Via de' Burro** on the far side of the square, make your way to the **Piazza di Pietra**, built along the side of remains of the Temple of Hadrian, now the Chamber of Commerce. If you are flagging, pause at **La Caffettiera**, one of the most elegant cafés in the city, which serves excellent Neapolitan coffee and pastries (particularly the sfogliatella napolitana). Leave the square at the far end, looking up at the magnificent altana of the **Palazzo Cini** (covered terraces designed to catch cool breezes in summer), and then almost immediately right up the **Via della Guglia**.

❿ At the end, past a somewhat patched obelisk, you will find yourself facing the bland **Palazzo Montecitorio**, now the Italian Parliament. To the right of this is the imposing **Palazzo Chigi**, official residence of the Prime Minister, looking out on the column of Marcus Aurelius (Emperor 161-180 AD). This is not as finely worked as Trajan's column, nor as well preserved, but it is a fascinating survival in the centre of the city that details the emperor's triumphs over various nations of eastern Europe.

⓫ Crossing back over the Corso, bear left, past the large shopping arcade, over the end of the **Via del Tritone**, into the **Piazza di S. Silvestro** and make towards the church of **S. Silvestro** over on the far side (next to the Post Office). The entrance is a charming courtyard lined with classical fragments, and while the interior is slightly gloomy, the church is full of fine 17thC paintings. If you like relics, enter the chapel on the left, where the head of John the Baptist is displayed. Although black and shrivelled, it is much adored, judging by the faithful crowds usually found in prayer (visitors are also drawn by the tragic statue of Mary holding the dead Jesus opposite). Emerge by this chapel into the **Via Belsiana**.

⓬ Follow this to the second street running at right angles, the **Via Frattina**, turn left and cross the Corso again. To the right runs the majestic façade of the **Palazzo Ruspoli**, and ahead is the elegant and blessedly traffic-free **Piazza S. Lorenzo in Lucina**. This takes its name from the church on the

Sign marking flood of December 1870 in S. Lorenzo in Lucina.

Palazzo Chigi.

left, evidently very old; the exterior dates from the 13th century, but the inside suffered major rebuilding in the 19th century and is sadly quite ordinary. It's worth entering, however, as there are one or two fine works of art, notably Bernini's *Bust of Dr Gabriele Fonseca* (in the fourth chapel on the left) and *The Crucifixion* by Guido Reni over the altar, oozing suffering. In the square, there are various bars and cafés – perhaps the best are **Teichner** (no. 15) and **Ciampini** (no. 29), more expensive and elegant, with superb ice-creams.

Bernini's bust of Dr Gabriele Fonseca S. Lorenzo in Lucina.

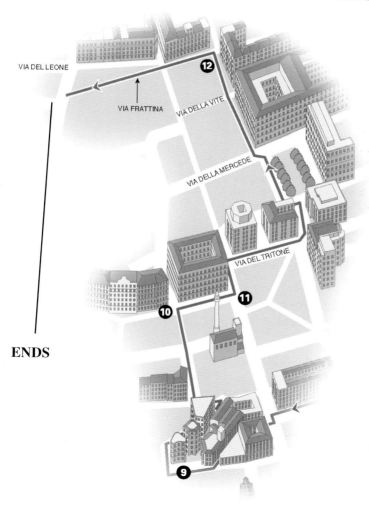

VIA DEL LEONE

VIA FRATTINA VIA DELLA VITE

VIA DELLA MERCEDE

VIA DEL TRITONE

ENDS

As Roman as it Comes: Around Campo de' Fioro

This fairly short walk loops round, ending where it began and taking you through what was once the commercial heart of the medieval city – many of the streets are named after the trades practised there (nails, combs, jerkins, barbers and so on). It was also a residential area, where there were inns for travellers and small houses for the middle classes, alongside very grand palaces. It was through here that papal processions on their way from St John Lateran to the Vatican would move in stately formation, alongside vast numbers of pilgrims. You will pass several fine Renaissance palaces including the finest in the city, a patch or two of ancient Rome, a few churches, two buildings with famous opera connections, and of course some lovely squares and fountains. The Campo de' Fiori itself starts the day as a market, but in the afternoon is cleared and cleaned and the bars and restaurants all the way round come into their own, as this is one of the most popular meeting points for the young of the city. There is no shortage of life here, but there are as some quiet corners if that is what you like.

▶ **STARTS**
Largo Torre Argentina.

■ **ENDS**
Largo Torre Argentina.
Nearest metro stop: Colosseo (2 km away, but there are many bus services running through Corso Vittorio Emanuele).

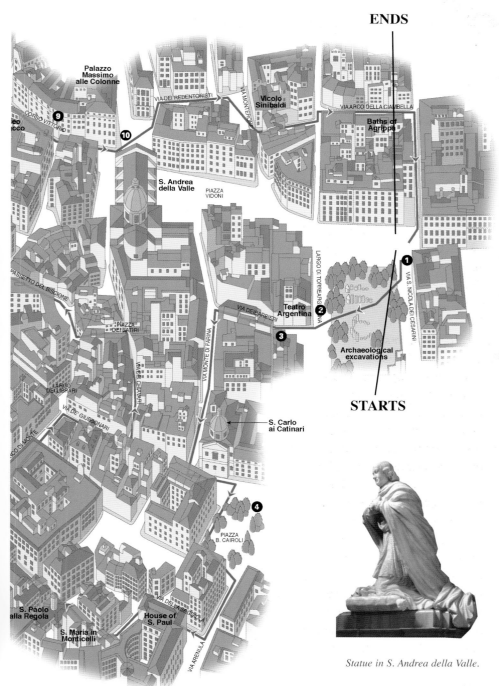

ENDS

Palazzo
Massimo
alle Colonne

VIA DEI REDENTORISTI

Vicolo
Sinibaldi

VIA ARCO DELLA CIAMBELLA

Baths of
Agrippa

CORSO VITTORIO

9

10

VIA MONTERONE

S. Andrea
della Valle

PIAZZA
VIDONI

VICOLO DEL BISCIONE

1

VIA S. NICOLA DEI CESARINI

LARGO DI TORRE ARGENTINA

VIA DEI BARBIERI

Teatro
Argentina

2

3

PIAZZA
DEI SATIRI

VIA MONTE DI FARINA

Archaeological
excavations

STARTS

LARGO
DEI LIBRARI

VIA DEI CHIAVARI

VIA DE' GIUBBONARI

S. Carlo
ai Catinari

ARCO DI MONTE

4

PIAZZA
B. CAIROLI

VIA DELLA SEGGIOLA

S. Paolo
alla Regola

House of
S. Paul

S. Maria in
Monticelli

VIA ARENULA

Statue in S. Andrea della Valle.

101

❶ Starting in the **Via S. Nicola dei Cesarini**, which runs along one side of the **Largo di Torre Argentina** (nothing to do with the country Argentina – the name derives from the Latin for Strasburg, Argentoratum), have a quick look at the excavations in the middle of the square. As the oldest surviving ruins from ancient Rome – some parts date to the 3rd century BC – they are archaelogically very important. However, there is nothing of real beauty here, and little of interest except perhaps to a specialist. There is no access either; the remains can only be viewed from above.

❷ Over on the other side of the square is a whitish building, the **Teatro Argentina**, topped by muses. It opened in 1732 and it's most glorious moment (with hindsight) was when the world première of Rossini's Barber of Seville was staged here on 20 February 1816. The actual première was a fiasco, reportedly because a black cat (bad luck in Italy) ran across the stage during the performance. Luckily, the next evening was better and the opera went on to enjoy great lasting success.

❸ Leave the square by way of the **Via dei Barbieri** (Barbers) to the left of the of the theatre. Tucked into a battered old palace at no. 7 on the left side of this street, is one of Rome's temples of modern design, **Spazio 7**. Then turn left along the **Via Monte di Farina** and follow this to the end, to the side of a huge church, **S. Carlo ai Catinari**, dating to the first half of the 17th century and dedicated to S. Carlo Borromeo, a descendent of one of Milan's grandest aristocratic families. Inside is a bit gloomy, but there are various frescoes and paintings by first-rate painters (such as Mattia Preti and Lanfranco) depicting scenes from his life – for instance,

Muses atop the Teatro Argentina.

over the main altar we see him marching along in *S. Carlo Carrying the Holy Nail in Procession during the Plague* (by Pietro da Cortona). Not to be missed is the Chapel of St Cecilia, last on the right, theatrically designed by Antonio Gherardi (1692-1700), in which angels peer down from a heavenly balcony.

Above, sculpted column on the façade of S. Carlo ai Catinari.

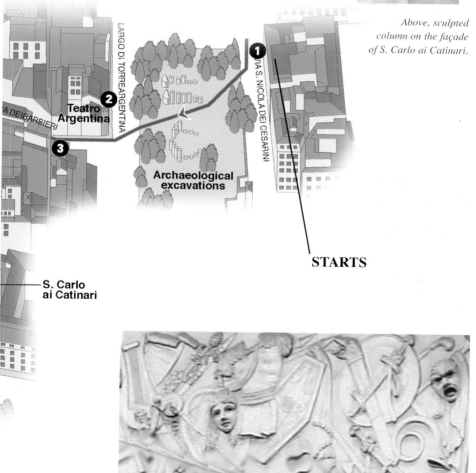

STARTS

S. Carlo ai Catinari

Dramatic relief work on the Teatro Argentine.

❹ In front of the church is a rather unattractive small public garden, with no grass and too many animals. Take the street up the side of this, turn left towards the **Via Arenula**, where the trams run, then right and soon right again into the **Via della Seggiola**. Here, at no. 12 is the modest **Bar Pica** which undoubtedly sells the best icecream in town. At the end of the street, bear left in front of the little church of **S. Maria in Monticelli**, and then past the excessively restored medieval house, so restored in fact that it seems almost Disneyland. Known as the **House of S. Paul**, it is supposedly built on the spot where the saint had his first Roman residence. Bearing right, you will see the church of **S. Paolo alla Regola** (pass) and then of **SS. Trinità dei Pellegrini** (pass), and then turn right down the **Via Arco di Monte** to the end. You will notice a plethora of small jewellers in these streets, the reason being that the great, gloomy block on the right was the Vatican pawn broking business (which still goes on, but in the hands of an Italian bank), and the jewellers were the spinoff. At the end is the **Via dei Giubbonari** (jerkin-makers), and across the street a small square, the **Largo dei Librari** (booksellers). At **no. 88** is written 'Filetti di baccalà', a much more famous institution than it looks, where they sell an approximation of fish and chips. The little church at the back, **S. Barbara** (patron saint of firemen), is decidedly pretty. Otherwise, right down the Via dei Giubbonari and first left along the **Via dei Chiavari** (keymakers) to the Piazza dei Satiri. The street to the left follows an unusual curved line, as the foundations of the buildings along it are the remains of the seating of one of Rome's largest theatres, the Theatre of Pompey (61-55 BC). It was at a meeting of the Senate in a chamber attached to the theatre that Julius Caesar was murdered on 15 March 44 BC . To the side of the little chapel in the street is a dark and usually rather smelly passageway, the **Passetto del Biscione**, but at the other end you emerge into light and bearing left come into the **Campo de' Fiori.** If you arrive in the morning, you will find a busy market. Once the square was filled with fruit and vegetable stores from end to end. A few still survive, alongside many more selling t-shirts and tat, but it remains colourful. By 2 pm all is cleared away and it then becomes one of the main drawing rooms of the city, a mass of humanity,

PASSETTO DEL BISCIONE

❺

Ruggeri

VIA DEI BALESTRARI

LARGO DEI LIBRARI

VIA DE' GIL

PIAZZA DELLA QUERCIA

Palazzo Spada

VIA ARCO DI MONTE

SS. Trinità dei Pellegrini

S. Paolo alla Regola

S. Maria Montic[

Palazzo Farnese façade.

foreign and local, idling away the day at one of the numerous bars all the way round.

❺ At no. 1/2 there is an old-fashioned foodstore, **Ruggeri**, an excellent place for prosciutto crudo, dried mushrooms etc, and to the side of it the **Via dei Balestrari** (sling makers), leading to the **Piazza della Quercia**. On the far side of this is a most striking, cream-coloured building, the **Palazzo Spada**, dating to 1548-50. The heavily moulded statues on the façade are figures from ancient Roman history, Augustus, Julius Caesar, Numa Pompilius, Romulus and so on (they are named). Passing through the handsome doors into the courtyard you will find the moulding continues, this time with mythological figures. There is a small and charming picture gallery in the building – no really outstanding paintings, but many very good ones displayed in attractive 17thC rooms. However, the most famous feature of the palace can be seen through the large window to the left of the courtyard – Borromini's *trompe l'oeil* colonnade, sometimes known as the 'Prospect of Borromini'. He was employed to restructure the palace in the 1630s and added this delightful folly. It is about nine metres long, but looks much more as the floor slopes up, the vault slopes down, the columns become rapidly shorter and closer together, all to give an illusion of length.

❻ Back in the street, turn left and you will see an enormous building looming ahead, the **Palazzo Farnese**. Before entering the square in front of it, stop a moment at the corner. From this point you can see both the façade and the side of the building. The block is of an astonishing size and beauty,and it is clear nothing was economized on in terms of scale and quality of design. In fact it took some seventy years to build (1517-89), and was the fruit of most of the finest architects working in Rome in that period, including Michelangelo, who was responsible for the cornice and much of the upper storey. The Farnese produced Pope Paul III, for whom Michelangelo painted *The Last Judgment* in the Sistine Chapel, and the family was almost indecently rich – while building this palace they were also putting up their country residence on almost the same scale (Palazzo Farnese at Caprarola – well-worth visiting). The square is also very beautiful, with its two fountains created from the largest Roman granite baths in existence.

❼ Heading for the restaurant in the corner, **Da Giovanni ar Galletto** (good Roman cuisine), and down the **Vicolo del Gallo**, across the end of the Campo de' Fiori, you will soon come to another enormous palace, the **Palazzo della Cancelleria** (1485-1513), originally a private home, but for centuries used by the Vatican as offices. Enter the stately courtyard, lined with columns taken from the Theatre of Pompey, and also the gloomy church in the corner of the building, **S. Lorenzo in Damaso**, to see the comically macabre funerary monument to the right of the entrance. A gaunt skeleton holds up a portrait of the deceased and taps him on the chin with a bony finger.

Palazzo della Cancelleria courtyard.

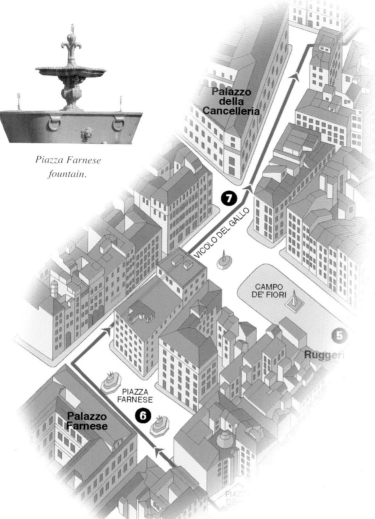

Piazza Farnese
fountain.

Palazzo
della
Cancelleria

7

VICOLO DEL GALLO

CAMPO
DE' FIORI

5

Ruggeri

PIAZZA
FARNESE

6

Palazzo
Farnese

Below, colourful market stalls in

Campo de'Fiori.

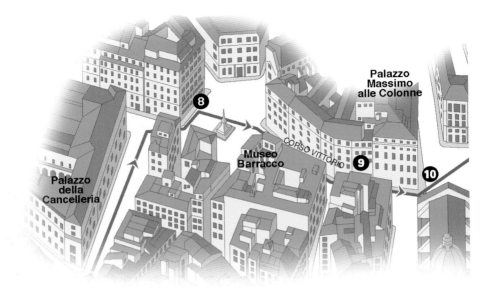

❽ Turning down the **Corso Vittorio**, you will very soon come to the little palace, the **Museo Barracco**. This small and exquisite archaeological collection was originally private, with some extraordinary items from Egypt, Babylon, Assyria, Palmyra, Greece and of course, Rome.

❾ Over on the other side of the street is the beautiful curving façade of the **Palazzo Massimo alle Colonne**, and on this side, a bit further on, is another enormous church, **S. Andrea della Valle** (1591-1650), the setting for the first act of Puccini's *Tosca*. The interior is lofty (the dome is the second highest after St Peter's), but all is bathed in an unattractive, yellow light and leaves a cold impression. The frescoes by Mattia Preti of the martyrdom of St Andrew on the walls of the apse and by Domenichino in the half dome are very fine. There is also an extraordinary display of coloured marbles in the first two chapels to the right of the entry, particularly the yellow-veined, black marble cenotaphs in the second.

❿ Cross over at the traffic lights, bear right to the corner of the square, down the **Via dei Redentoristi**, across the **Via Monterone**, under the sinister arch of **Vicolo Sinibaldi**, down the **Via Arco della Ciambella**, past the remains of the **Baths of Agrippa** (a fascinating example of housing embedded in classical remains), then right at the end, and back to where you started.

Pretty doorway on Via Monterone.

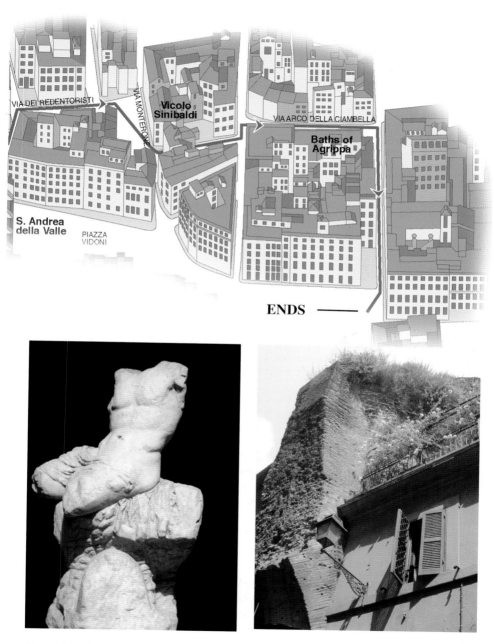

VIA DEI REDENTORISTI

VIA MONTERONE

Vicolo
Sinibaldi

VIA ARCO DELLA CIAMBELLA

Baths of
Agrippa

S. Andrea
della Valle

PIAZZA
VIDONI

ENDS ———

Statue of Apollo, courtyard of Museo Barracco.

Baths of Agrippa.

Counts and Pilgrims:
From Ponte Sisto to Ponte Sant' Angelo

Statues of Ponte Sant'Angelo with Castel Sant'Angelo behind.

▲ **STARTS**
Ottaviano–S. Pietro.
Nearest metro stop:
S. Pietro (2.4 km away).

■ **ENDS**
Ponte Sant' Angelo.
Nearest metro stop:
Lepanto.

Castel Sant' Angelo

FIUME TEVERE

Ponte Sant'Angelo

ENDS

9

LUNGOTEVERE TOR DI NONA

VIA DI MONTE GIORDANO

Palazzo Taverna

VIA DI PANICO

VIA DEL CORALLO

PIAZZA DEL FICO

VIA DEL GOVERNO VECCHIO

Chiesa Nuova

Oratorio dei Filippini

CORSO VITTORIO EMANUELE II

Palazzo Sforza Cesarini

PIAZZA SFORZA

VICOLO CELLINI

San Giovanni Battista dei Fiorentini

Palazzo Sacchetti

6

Sant'Agnese in Agone

PIAZZA NAVONA

Fountain of the Four Rivers

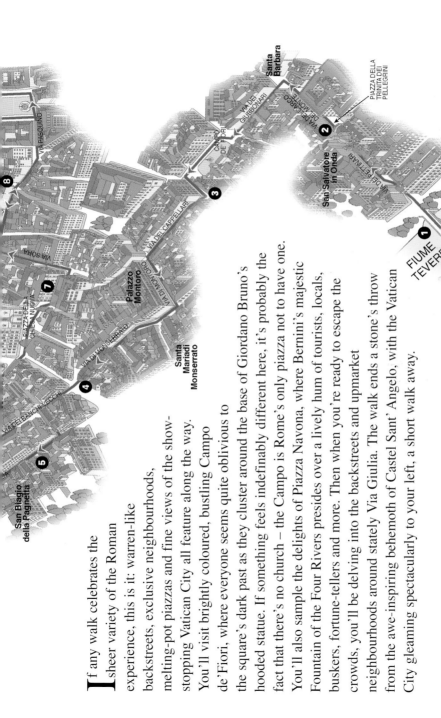

STARTS

I f any walk celebrates the sheer variety of the Roman experience, this is it: warren-like backstreets, exclusive neighbourhoods, melting-pot piazzas and fine views of the show-stopping Vatican City all feature along the way. You'll visit brightly coloured, bustling Campo de'Fiori, where everyone seems quite oblivious to the square's dark past as they cluster around the base of Giordano Bruno's hooded statue. If something feels indefinably different here, it's probably the fact that there's no church – the Campo is Rome's only piazza not to have one. You'll also sample the delights of Piazza Navona, where Bernini's majestic Fountain of the Four Rivers presides over a lively hum of tourists, locals, buskers, fortune-tellers and more. Then when you're ready to escape the crowds, you'll be delving into the backstreets and upmarket neighbourhoods around stately Via Giulia. The walk ends a stone's throw from the awe-inspiring behemoth of Castel Sant' Angelo, with the Vatican City gleaming spectacularly to your left, a short walk away.

Map labels:
PIAZZA DELLA TRINITÀ DEI PELLEGRINI
Santa Barbara
VIA DEI GIUBBONARI
VIA DE' MONTI
CAMPO DE' FIORI
San Salvatore in Onda
VIA DE' PETTINARI
Ponte Sisto
FIUME TEVERE
VIA DEL CAPPELLARI
VIA DI MONSERRATO
VIA MONTORO
Palazzo Montoro
Santa Maria di Monserrato
VIA SORA
PIAZZA DELLA CHIESA NUOVA
VIA DEI BANCHI VECCHI
San Biagio della Pagnetta
VIA DI PASQUINO

1 2 3 4 5 7 8

❶ Ponte Sisto is Rome's first papal bridge, built in 1474 by Pope Sixtus IV on the site of Marcus Aurelius's Pons Aurelianus. The Gianicolo hills rise to the west and St Peter's dominates the horizon to the north – you'll end up just shy of the Vatican on this walk. The Tiber is elegant here, within high stone walls (inevitably grafittied) and flanked by wide footpaths. Walk over to the east (Colosseum) side of the river and cross the busy road at the end to walk down **Via dei Pettinari**. On your left is pretty **San Salvatore in Onda**, a 12thC church containing the body of St Vincent Pallotti in a sarcophagus under the main altar. There is a charming arcaded nave (look for the lovely flower paintings on the undersides of the arches, made to look like mosaics), a beautiful ceiling and unusual stained glass windows.

❷ Continuing onwards, you soon come to **Piazza della Trinita dei Pellegrini**. Keep going ahead along **Via dell'Arco del Monte** until you come to **Via dei Giubbonari**, with dainty little **Santa Barbara** in front of you. Turn left along Via dei Giubbonari, 'street of the jacket makers', and a couple of minutes' walk brings you to the **Campo de'Fiori**. Once a stage for public executions, the Piazza is now Rome's most vibrant food market, with a small town atmosphere and a host of alluring shops. There's the inevitable tat as well – you can't escape those 'I Heart Roma' hoodies – but it all just adds to the colour. The hooded figure of Renaissance sceptic Giordano Bruno, who was burnt alive here in 1600 under orders of the Inquisition, looms over the square as a reminder of its dark history.

❸ Opposite the road by which you entered is medieval **Via del Cappellari**. Go down this until **Via di Montoro** crosses and turn left. This is an interesting street because of the unusual lintels over the windows of **Palazzo Montoro**: clean, simple carved lines

and some sweet fake painted windows above them. Turn right when you come to **Via di Monserrato**, with the Spanish national church, **Santa Maria di Monserrato**, in front of you. Here lies Alfonso XIII, the last king of pre-Civil War Spain. Continue past blocks of elegant apartments – the whole street has a refined, luxurious feel, despite the occasional graffiti. There are some

Santa Mariadi Monserrato

delightful high-quality art galleries, not interested in pleasing tourists, a sure sign of an upmarket area.

Shop sign along Via di Monserrato

Santa Barbara.

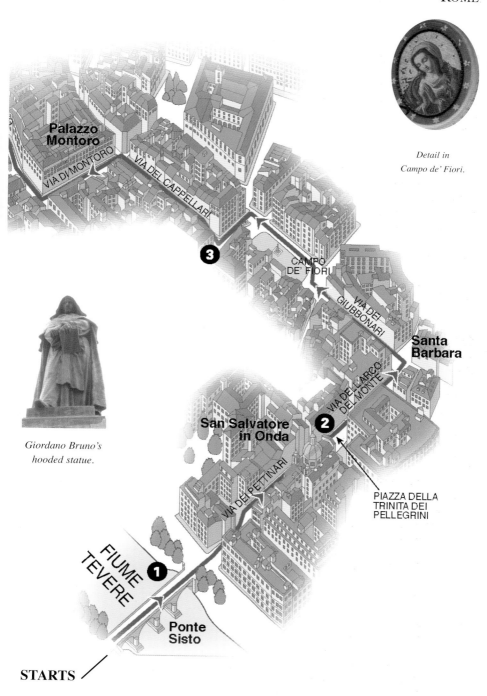

ROME

*Detail in
Campo de' Fiori.*

Palazzo
Montoro

VIA DI MONTORO

VIA DEL CAPPELLARI

❸

CAMPO
DE' FIORI

VIA DEI
GIUBBONARI

Santa
Barbara

*Giordano Bruno's
hooded statue.*

San Salvatore
in Onda

VIA DELL'ARCO
DEL MONTE

❷

VIA DEI PETTINARI

PIAZZA DELLA
TRINITA DEI
PELLEGRINI

FIUME
TEVERE

❶

Ponte
Sisto

STARTS

113

❹ The road leads into an open square and then becomes **Via dei Banchi Vecchi**. Just after the church, turn left as far as **Via Giulia** and then turn right. Opened in the early decades of the 1600s, under the orders of Pope Julius II, this 1 km thoroughfare was the city's first grand gesture in road building since the days of the Roman Empire. Flanked by noble palazzi, it was part of the Pope's masterplan to create a fitting approach to St Peter's, and was Renaissance Rome's most prestigious address. Lined with opulent antique shops and art galleries, it is still one of the most exclusive residential areas in the city. Each store has its own red, emblazoned flag, which gives the whole place a regal air. This street is an appropriate monument to Julius II, a great patron of the arts who commissioned the painting of the Sistine Chapel.

❺Pass **San Biagio della Pagnetta** on your left, dedicated to St Blaise, patron saint of wild animals and those with throat problems. Every year, the Armenian monks hand out loaves of bread (pagnetta) to the faithful on 3rd February, St Blaise's feast day. Continue along Via Giulia, passing the enormous door of 16thC **Palazzo Sacchetti**, and you will come to **Piazza dell'Oro**, with the cream cake confection of **San Giovanni Battista dei Fiorentini** on your left. This 16thC church was commissioned by Pope Leo X (of the Florentine Medici clan), as a showcase of Florentine talent, though it was not actually finished until the 1730s. Unusually, animals are allowed to attend services here and an annual lamb-blessing ceremony takes place at Easter.

San Giovanni
Battista dei
Fiorentini

Palazzo
Sacchetti

San Bia
della Pagne

Above, figures above the doorway of San Giovanni Battista, and right, one of the sculptural panels flanking the entrance.

CLEMENS·XII·PONT·MAX·A·S·MDCCXXXIV·P·IV

VIA GIULIA
1508
Laboratorio

bikesharing

Top, inscription on San Giovanni Battista. Left, a flag hanging outside a boutique on Via Guilia and right, bike-sharing outside the church.

CORSO

VICOLO SUGARELLI

VIA GIULIA

Palaz
Sforz
Cesarin

VIA DEI BANCHI VECCHI

gio
tta

5

4

VIA DI MONSERRATO

Santa
Mariadi
Monserrato

115

6 Retrace your steps back down Via Giulia and turn left down **Vicolo Sugarelli**. A right turn at the end takes you back on to **Via dei Banchi Vecchi** and the back of **Palazzo Sforza Cesarini**. It was built for Rodrigo Borgia, the future Pope Alexander VI, who is said to have sold it for the price of Cardinal Ascanio Sforza's vote in the papal Conclave. Turn left down **Vicolo Sforza Cesarini** and you will come to the piazza of the same name. The mother of the infamous Cesare and Lucrezia Borgia lived at **no. 27**, and the pair may well have been born here. Turn right out of the Piazza on to **Corso Vittorio Emanuele II** and keep going till you reach **Piazza della Chiesa Nuova**, a spacious square scattered with benches (these are few and far between in Rome, so take the opportunity to rest your feet). The building to the left of the church is the **Oratorio dei Fillipini**, Rome's oldest public library, where the musical form of the oratorio was developed. Next door, in the **Chiesa Nuova**, there are three fine paintings by Rubens around the altar.

7 Continue onwards and soon turn left down the pretty **Via Sora**, to emerge on to **Via del Governo Vecchio**. A right turn here, then keeping straight ahead through **Piazza Pasquino** and along **Via Pasquino**, takes you to famous **Piazza Navona**, one of the finest Baroque jewels in Rome's crown. It preserves the distinctive shape of Domitian's stadium of AD 96, and where crowds once gathered to watch sports, they now do so for coffee and ice cream in the dozens of cafés which ring the square. If you fancy something to eat, it's worth having a look around first, as prices vary. The piazza's current appearance is courtesy of Pope Innocent X who, seeking to enhance the family name, Pamphilj, commissioned the great architects of his day to

San Giovanni Battista dei Fiorentini

6

CORSO VITTORIO EMANUELE II

Palazzo Sacchetti

VICOLO SUGARELLI

VIA DEI BANCHI VECCHI

Palazzo Sforza Cesarini

PIAZZA SFORZA CESARINI

VIA DEL BANCHI VECCHI

Oratorio dei Fillipini

PIAZZA CHIESA

San Biagio

Piazza Navona.

in the church of San Giovanni Battista di Fiorentini (which you passed soon after point ❺), despite his death by suicide. He designed the Falconieri chapel there, and is interred within the family tomb of Carlo Maderno, another architect and a distant relation, who oversaw much of the construction of the church.

Detail along Corso Vittori Emanuele.

make the piazza in front of his family home into a fitting memorial for his reign. Bernini's **Fountain of the Four Rivers** (1651) is the Piazza's crowning glory: colossal figures representing the Nile, Danube, Ganges and Plate hold up an ancient Roman obelisk, recovered from the Circus Maxentius. Pope Innocent is buried in **Sant'Agnese in Agone**, the glorious church next door to the **Palazzo Pamphilj**. The façade of the church is by leading Baroque architect Borromini, who is buried

Chiesa Nuova

VIA DEL CORALLO

VIA DEL GOVERNO VECCHIO

DELLA NUOVA

❼

VIA SORA

Sant'Agnese in Agone

PIAZZA NAVONA

VIA PASQUINO

Fountain of the Four Rivers

8 Retrace your steps to Via Sora on the left and continue along **Vicolo del Governo Vecchio**, with its vintage shops and useful supermarket. Turn right on to **Via del Corallo**, which quickly becomes **Piazza del Fico**. Turn left on to **Vicolo del Fico**, a pretty street with flowers in the windows, and then left on to **Via di Monte Giordano**, following it as it curves round to the right past a couple of pizzerias. There's a friendly, local feel to this area, and you might want to stop for some lunch. Go past lofty **Palazzo Taverna** on your right, one-time palace of the forceful Orsini family and said to be built on the site of Rome's first amphitheatre. The road turns into **Via di Panico**, a charming, colourful street lined with interesting little shops. Emerge on to **Lungotevere Tor di Nona** and cross over for **Ponte Sant' Angelo** and spectacular views of the **Castel Sant' Angelo**.

9 Ponte Sant' Angelo is still supported by three of the original arches of Emperor Hadrian's Pons Aelius.
Look down to your right and under the modern embankments are the remains of the wharfs where the great monoliths of marble needed to build Imperial Rome were unloaded. Lovely, graceful angels by Baroque's blue-eyed-boy Bernini (he of the Fountain of the Four Rivers) escort you across the bridge into the towering presence of fortress Castel Sant' Angelo. Thomas Hobbes, the 17thC philosopher, described the papacy as 'the ghost

Statue on Ponte Sant'Angelo.

of the deceased Roman Empire sitting crowned upon the grave thereof'. This takes on a chilling resonance here: the fortress that witnessed so many of the excesses of the powerful medieval popes was originally the mausoleum of the Emperor Hadrian. Begun in AD 130, it houses the ashes of succeeding Roman emperors until Septimius Severus. The castle itself, at least from the waist down, is still essentially Hadrian's, though the lavish marble cladding has long

St. Peter's from Ponte Sant'Angelo.

Ponte Sant'Angelo.

since gone. Inside, an ancient ramp still leads up to his funerary chamber, while above you can visit the luxurious Papal apartments. The bronze angel on its pinnacle and the castle's name record Pope Gregory the Great's vision of an angel sheathing its bloody sword that marked the end of the plague in AD 590. The castle also enjoyed notoriety as a prison: Giordano Bruno was held here before he was burnt to death in the Campo de' Fiori; metalsmith, author and general Renaissance man Benvenuto Cellini managed to escape with only a broken leg. Tosca was less successful: she brings Puccini's opera of the same name to a close by throwing herself off the battlements. From the Castle, a left turn down **Borgo San Angelo** or **Via della Conciliazione** takes you into the **Vatican City**.

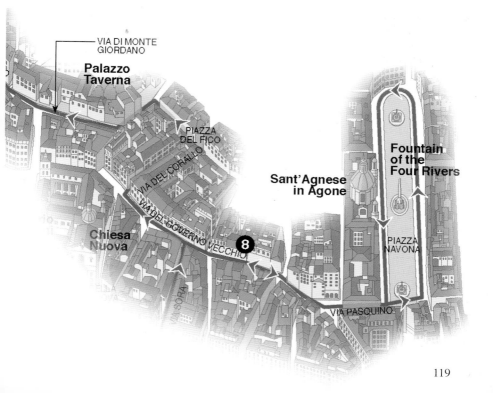

VIA DI MONTE GIORDANO

Palazzo Taverna

PIAZZA DEL FICO

VIA DEL CORALLO

Chiesa Nuova

VIA DEL GOVERNO VECCHIO

VIA SORA

❽

Sant'Agnese in Agone

Fountain of the Four Rivers

PIAZZA NAVONA

VIA PASQUINO

The Other Romans: Meandering around Trastevere

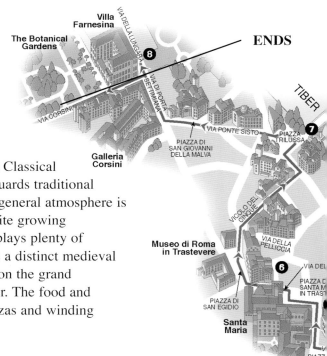

The ancient cosmopolitan district of Trastevere lies on the opposite bank of the river to the rest of the city – its name translates as 'across the Tiber' – and it really does have that 'other side of the river' feel to it. Where central Rome safeguards Classical culture, Trastevere safeguards traditional popular culture, and the general atmosphere is buzzy and relaxed. Despite growing gentrification, it still displays plenty of romantic neglect and has a distinct medieval vibe, having missed out on the grand renovations over the river. The food and nightlife around the piazzas and winding backstreets are great.

Map labels: Villa Farnesina, The Botanical Gardens, VIA DELLA LUNGARA, **ENDS**, VIA DI PORTA SETTIMIANA, VIA CORSINI, TIBER, VIA PONTE SISTO, PIAZZA TRILUSSA ❼, PIAZZA DI SAN GIOVANNI DELLA MALVA, Galleria Corsini, ❽, ❼, VICOLO DEL CINQUE, Museo di Roma in Trastevere, VIA DELLA PELLICCIA, ❻, VIA DEL, PIAZZA D SANTA M IN TRAST, PIAZZA DI SAN EGIDIO, Santa Maria, PIAZZ DI SAN CALIST

The Botanical Gardens.

Along Via dei Fienaroli.

Historically multicultural – in Republican times it was home to the Jewish and Syrian communities, as well as various sailors, soldiers, slaves and summering noblemen – Trastevere is a mix of styles and influences: grand palazzi rub shoulders with humble, ivy-clad houses, and flapping laundry is slung casually from one side of the street to the other. The Trasteverini – the local inhabitants, who regard themselves as 'true' Romans – sun themselves in doorways and in the squares.

You're not just visiting for the ambience, though – Trastevere has beautiful churches, buildings and monuments to compete with the best of them. Santa Cecilia and Santa Maria in Trastevere are masterpieces of design, each filled with hidden treasures and intriguing back-stories. You will end up at the lovely, verdant Botanical Gardens – after following this route, you'll enjoy getting lost there.

▶ **STARTS**
Ponte Cestio, south side of the river. Nearest metro stop: Circo Massimo.

■ **ENDS**
The Botanical Gardens
Nearest metro stop: S. Pietro (2.3 km away).

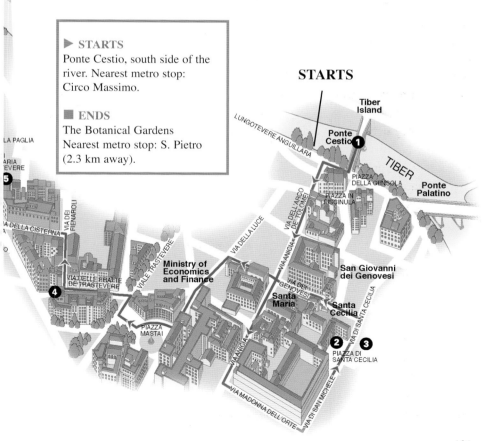

❶ With **Tiber Island** over the bridge to your left, walk a very short distance down **Lungotevere Anguillara**. (For a walk that includes Tiber Island itself, see the 'Two Islands' walk, page 42.) Immediately on your left is **Piazza della Gensola**, between a pretty pink, walled house on the left and a grander yellow block on the right. Turn left down this wide street, which opens up into **Piazza in Piscinula**, a typical Trastevere mix of buzzing restaurants, medieval palazzi and a sprinkling of antique fragments. Continue straight ahead on to **Via dell'Arco de'Tolomei**, which turns into **Via Anicia**, and then take the third street on the left, **Via Madonna dell'Orte**. The deserted backstreets with their industrial flavour are a far cry from the gracious streets of central Rome, but it's all part of the experience of Trastevere. At the end, turn left down the **Via di San Michele**, and in a matter of footsteps you've moved from dingy roads to the elegant **Piazza di Santa Cecilia**, surrounded by sweet houses. There's unlikely to be another tourist in sight.

❷ The courtyard of **Santa Cecilia** is cool, symmetrical and inviting, and the same goes for the church's interior. If you are a little tired of the Baroque excess found all over Rome, **Santa Maria**'s graceful white curves are a pleasant antidote. The original building is 9thC (though it has extensive additions), and is constructed over the house of martyred Saint Cecilia, the patron saint of musicians. This is believed to be the place of her death – she was first suffocated

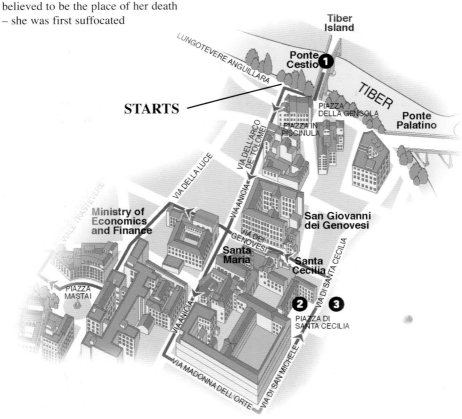

in her own bath and then, when this failed to kill her, attacked with axe blows to the neck. She died three days later. She was found with three fingers outstretched on one hand, and on the other just one finger, denoting her belief in the Trinity. When she was exhumed in 1599, the sculptor Stefano Maderno was present, and he produced in response the moving statue in front of the choir. The figure's uncomfortable position is unnervingly human – no classical poses here. Inscribed on the round marble slab is the sculptor's oath that Saint Cecilia's body was found intact. The excavated house below the church and Pietro Cavallini's beautiful fresco *The Last Judgement* are open at selected times during the day (ring 06-5899289 for details).

❸ Coming out of the courtyard, turn left along **Via di Santa Cecilia**. Look out for a leather shop on your left, and don't be put off by the knick-knacks in the window – it's a proper craftsman's workshop, and a useful place to buy good-value gifts not of the miniature Colosseum variety. Turn almost immediately left again on to **Via dei Genovesi** and keep going past the large cream-coloured church on your right. This is **San Giovanni dei Genovesi**, a hospice built to care for the Genoese sailors disembarking at the nearby port of Ripa Grande. When you reach **Via della Luce**, turn left and continue until it opens into **Piazza Mastai**, dominated by the neo-Classical Ministry of Economics and Finance. Leave the piazza opposite the way you came in and cross **Viale**

Pretty shop on Santa Maria.

Trastevere. Turn right and soon left down **Via delle Fratte de Trastevere**. The big structure in the distance, at the end of the street, is the fountain that marks the end of the **Acqua Paola aqueduct**. The aqueducts were one of the Emperor Trajan's building projects. This fountain was built in the 1610s, to celebrate Pope Paul V's restoration of the Roman waterway.

On Via Anicia.

Santa Cecilia.

❹ Shortly turn right down **Via dei Fienaroli** and then left down **Via della Cisterna**. Just before you emerge into **Piazza di San Calisto**, look for the quirky drinking fountain with two wine flasks and a barrel spouting water. Unfortunately the graffiti which covers the whole of Trastevere makes the bubbling water look less than inviting – save yourself for **Piazza di Santa Maria**, which has any number of watering holes. (However, it's worth noting that if you want to eat around Trastevere, it's best to steer clear of the main squares, where some of the restaurants take advantage of tourists.) Piazza di San Calisto is a bustling little square, a taste of the greater bustle just round the corner in Santa Maria – turn right and follow the noise.

❺ Piazza di Santa Maria in Trastevere is a jolly place, with teeming restaurants, interesting shops and lively buskers. The octagonal fountain in the middle of the square is always crowded with tourists and locals alike, soaking up the sun and the atmosphere. On a summer's evening you really feel as if you are in the pulsing heart of Trastevere – it's a very different experience from the average tourist's Rome, which can sometimes feel like something of a marketing construct. **Santa Maria** is the earliest church in the city dedicated to the cult of the Virgin – there has been a church here since the early 3rd century, though the present structure dates from 1138. The mosaics on the façade glow warmly in the sunshine, and the lovely Romanesque bell tower strikes every 15 minutes. Inside, the gold-gilted church glows still more, softly illuminating a fabulous apsidal mosaic by Cavallini (the use of perspective was groundbreaking for the time) and an elegant marble-columned nave. To the right of the altar the inscription '*fons olei*' marks the spot where a fountain of oil was said to burst from the ground in 38 BC, later interpreted by Christians as a sign of the coming of the Messiah.

Inside Santa Maria.

Pretty house on Via dei Fienaroli.

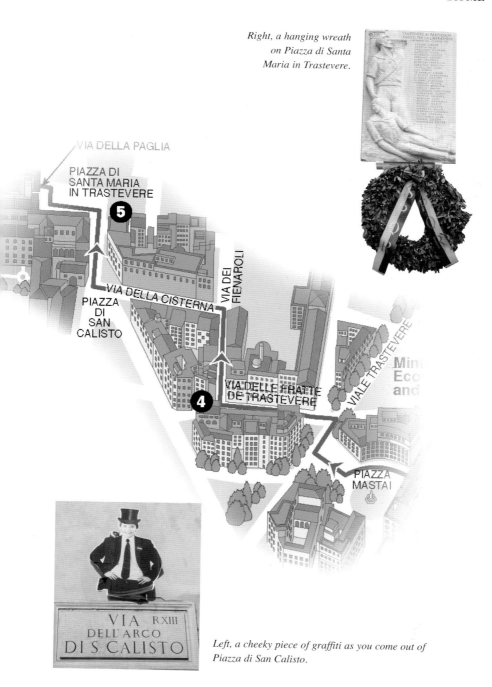

Right, a hanging wreath on Piazza di Santa Maria in Trastevere.

VIA DELLA PAGLIA

PIAZZA DI SANTA MARIA IN TRASTEVERE

5

VIA DELLA CISTERNA

VIA DEI FIENAROLI

PIAZZA DI SAN CALISTO

VIA DELLE FRATTE DE TRASTEVERE

4

VIALE TRASTEVERE

Min Eco and

PIAZZA MASTAI

VIA RXIII DELL'ARCO DI S CALISTO

Left, a cheeky piece of graffiti as you come out of Piazza di San Calisto.

6 Leaving the church, turn left and left again down **Via della Paglia**, which opens into **Piazza di San Egidio**. Turn right into the piazza, past the **Museo di Roma in Trastevere** on your left. It is appropriate to the spirit of the area that the museum is focused on folklore, daily life in the 18th and 19th centuries, and the Roman dialect poets. If you are enjoying hoping to explore a different 'type' of Rome to the white-marbled classical one, it's well worth a visit. Go down **Via della Pelliccia** a short way and branch right at the crossroads down **Vicolo del Cinque**, a cute backstreet lined with little restaurants. The road ends at the **Piazza Trilussa**, where a left turn uphill takes you back to the river, past an impressive fountain set high in a Baroque portico on your left.

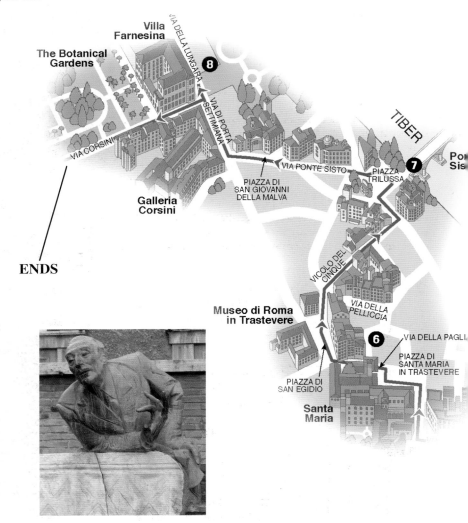

Statue of Roman dialect poet Trilussa.